Skyhorse Publishing books may be purchased in bulk at special discounts for sales promotion, corporate gifts, fund-raising, or educational purposes. Special editions can also be created to specifications. For details, contact the Special Sales Department, Skyhorse Publishing, 307 West 36th Street, 11th Floor, New York, NY 10018 or info@skyhorsepublishing.com.

Skyhorse® and Skyhorse Publishing® are registered trademarks of Skyhorse Publishing, Inc.®, a Delaware corporation.

Visit our website at www.skyhorsepublishing.com.

10 9 8 7 6 5 4 3 2 1

Library of Congress Cataloging-in-Publication Data is available on file.

ISBN: 978-1-62087-201-7

Printed in China

FABULOUS
RAW FOOD

Erica Palmcrantz Aziz

Photographer Anna Hult

FABULOUS RAW FOOD

Translation by Lena Golden

DETOX, LOSE WEIGHT, AND FEEL GREAT IN JUST THREE WEEKS!

SKYHORSE PUBLISHING

CONTENTS

Welcome to a Lighter Life!

It has been seven years since I started the raw food diet, and I am still surprised by how much it does for me. The first things I noticed when I started eating raw were an increase in my energy level, a balanced blood sugar level, and a more settled stomach. I dropped a few pounds and my thoughts became more positive. Raw food became a big part of my life, and since then I have been a happier person and my daily living has become simpler in many ways. And now I want to share this with you!

Before I started with raw food, I had tried various diets and programs without any satisfaction or joy. When I was eighteen, I went on a diet called "the metabolic cure." I wasn't a coffee drinker, but according to the diet I was supposed to start the day with a cup of coffee with sugar. By ten o'clock I would be shaking, partly because of hunger, and partly because of the caffeine. For lunch, I was supposed to eat half of a grilled chicken and that was it. In retrospect, I realize how crazy that was. Today, I don't even remember why I started that regimen, but I do remember that it was twelve days of pure torture.

That and my experience with other similar programs are what led me to write this book, along with the fact that I met so many people curious about raw food since my books *Raw Food* and *Raw Desserts* came out. I hope this book will inspire you to make an enjoyable and sustainable change in your lifestyle.

By eating clean, nutritious food that is tasty and prepared in a simple fashion with organic ingredients, you can help your body get back into its natural balance. You will have an opportunity to discover exactly what it is that you need to feel good. Feeling good is also about achieving a balance in meeting all the needs in life. Sleep, exercise, thirst, hunger, and emotions—all these areas should be taken into account.

Raw food is food made from vegetables, fruits, nuts, seeds, sprouts, shoots, and sea vegetables. Honey, cold pressed oils, and superfoods are also used. In order to preserve the life energy and a maximum of nutrition, dishes are prepared by mixing rather than by heating. It is also possible to dehydrate or heat in a double boiler to a maximum of 104°F (40°C).

Through simple self-reflective exercises, you can become more aware of your real needs and build a solid foundation for new habits that will make you feel great.

I have put together detox programs for one, three, seven, and twenty-one days so that you can choose the plan that's right for you to cleanse and get a fresh start. To be able to follow through with the desired number of detox days, you have to have the right mindset and be patient. It's not always going to be easy, and you will have to find motivation from within. What you are doing now is something good for your body. When we do things for ourselves out of sheer love rather than just trying to get to the finish line, that's when we can really change for the better.

In this book, you will also get to know Maria and Jeanine, two women who tried my three-week program. They share their experiences with raw food and the changes it made to their lifestyles.

Before you read any further, I would like to share a thought with you. I watch children's movies with my daughter, Saga, and some of the movies have such beautiful messages. One of our favorite movies is *Tinkerbell,* about a fairy who helps a little girl and her father get back together. In the movie she sprinkles her magical *pixie dust* over them, which enables the girl and her father to fly and see life from a different perspective. This makes me think of how a change in lifestyle gives you the opportunity to look at life in a dramatically new way. So now I would sprinkle a little *pixie dust* on you to propel you toward the life you really want to live!

Go raw . . . your way!
Erica

P.S. At the back of the book you will find a picture of a pair of bare feet in the green summer grass. The picture reminds me to take one step at a time, to be curious about how each new step feels, and at the same time to feel our magic earth safely under our feet.

About the Author

Erica Palmcrantz Aziz is thirty-four years old and lives in Gothenburg, Sweden, with her husband, Sam, and their daughter, Saga, who is four years old. Erica is passionate about raw food and inspires people to find their own way to eat and live with raw food through her lectures and books. She lives as a "high raw vegan," which means that about 85 percent of her diet consists of raw food. When Erica is not busy inspiring others to try raw food, she enjoys being outdoors with her family, reading, practicing yoga, and trying out new recipes in her kitchen.

What I like best about the raw detox: "Taking a step back from everyday life helps me to see what works and what doesn't work in my life. Periodically detoxing and replenishing with fresh energy makes it easier for me to discover what makes me feel my best."

Favorite recipe: "I love parsley, so my favorite dish would have to be parsley tabbouleh. For a snack or dessert, I'd go with tangy carrot cake—so fresh-tasting and yummy!"

Advice to others who want to try a raw detox:
"Find your inner motivation for making a lifestyle change and remind yourself of it every day. Try to keep it in mind when you're experiencing difficulties. Feel the joy of the investment you are making—for both your body and your mind."

A Lighter Life Creates Harmony.
Experience Change in Just Three Weeks!

This book is for those who want to live a lighter life physically and mentally. Spend a little time on yourself, detox, and make room for something new.

Long Live Life!

Body and Mind

Fabulous Raw Food is written for those of you who are looking for a lifestyle change rather than a temporary diet. It is a book you can return to at any time throughout your life to find new inspiration for a lighter life, both physically and mentally as you discover ways to restore communication between the two. Completing one of these programs will help you create new habits, tailored to you, for a better life.

Since I started with raw food, my weight has stayed the same, just fluctuating about five pounds depending on the season, my menstrual cycle, and how I feel emotionally. When I make choices that I know are the best for me, body weight is no longer the focus. Instead, I look for a sense of ease, simplicity, and fulfillment. All the energy that I used to spend thinking about what I could or could not eat can now be spent on other, happier thoughts. It is a win-win situation—both body and mind feel lighter.

Even if we eat super healthy foods, negative thoughts can sometimes weigh us down. I won't deny that, but I have noticed a connection between food that is heavy and indigestible and heavy, indigestible thoughts. Food that makes us slow and sluggish gives us less energy to think positively and thus makes it harder to reach our dreams and goals. Food should be joyful and a part of the good life!

To what degree do you want to cleanse yourself?
Both new research and ancient teachings say that it takes twenty-one days to form a new habit. Obviously this differs from one person to another—it may be faster or slower than that—but this is about the amount of time it takes to form habits that are more in line with what you want for your life. When attempting to make a lifestyle change, we must remember to be patient with

ourselves—we have probably had the old habit for several years. If you are unable to make a commitment to the twenty-one day program, then seven days is a good investment. If you are just a little bit curious, you can try for three days and then try for an extended period when you feel ready.

I do not recommend following the program week after week for several months. This may make you forget to tune in to what really makes YOU feel good. But you can always repeat the program periodically if you feel like you want an energy boost!

How will I feel when I start eating raw food?

- **On the days** that you eat raw food, you'll experience "fullness" in a different way. You will not experience the "food coma" that can set in after you eat a meal; instead, you'll just feel pleasantly satisfied. The lighter feeling of satiation makes you naturally hungry after three hours, and the body is then ready to take in more food. Most of us maintain a more balanced blood sugar level if we eat every three hours. Because the food contains live enzymes that help digestion, you will feel refreshed after a meal and you won't feel the need for coffee as a pick-me-up.

- **Your energy level** will increase. When I started with raw food, I had a hard time understanding and adapting to all the extra energy I had. These changes may vary, depending on your former diet and lifestyle. If you are used to drinking a lot of coffee, you may experience headaches the first few days, and if you normally eat a lot of sugars and simple carbohydrates, you may feel withdrawal symptoms such as headaches, fatigue, or nausea. If you experience any of these, rest, breathe, and drink plenty of water.

- **If you get a sudden craving** for something, stop and ask yourself why. Realizing why you are craving something may cause the craving to disappear, or it may be because you are actually lacking something you need. Exploring the cravings can be very interesting.

- **You may become** more regular than you used to be as your body cleanses. Or you may actually go to the bathroom less, as your intestines are not accustomed to the new, high-fiber diet. You can read more about this in the chapter "Being Regular."

- **You might lose weight,** which is discussed in more detail in the chapter "Is Body Weight Important?"

- **Once you start eating** foods that are more "pure," you may be more sensitive to the foods you ate before. By "pure" food, I mean natural ingredients that are not processed or refined and that are free from pesticides, additives, and trans fats.

- **You might find** that your body or mind is resisting change. Try to discover why this is. If you are on the program with a friend, remember to encourage each other. You can, for example, summarize and reflect on the days that have passed, what has been good, fun, or difficult. That may make the next day easier.

- **It never fails**—every time I detox through diet, I also clear out the clothes in my closet that I don't use. I organize my cabinets, clean, and fix things up. It seems that detoxing on the inside makes me want to clean and reorganize everything.

Do you want this?

Am I going to have time for this? Do I have what it takes? What if I'm going on a business trip? What will my co-workers say? It is easy to find excuses not to make a wholehearted effort. You simply have to make an agreement with yourself to make a full commitment.

You have to remember that food is only part of the program. Other factors in your daily life, such as TV, friends, news, gossip magazines, and the Internet, affect your mental and physical health more than you can imagine. You will choose to what extent you want to cleanse yourself. Maybe you should take the opportunity to spend less time surfing the Net? Maybe you need to clean out your closet? Or why not go to bed an hour earlier each night and see how that feels? Think about what brings you harmony in life. Be kind to yourself and remember that a sustainable change takes time to implement but is much better than a gimmicky diet that fails shortly after you start. Give yourself time and space to really feel what goes on during these weeks—honest reflection will create the foundation for sustainable change.

How to Use This Book!

- **Read the whole book** before you start so you can see the bigger picture of a lifestyle change.

- **By completing the exercises,** you will get a clearer picture of your motivations and goals.

- **Do read the recipes** beforehand and see which ingredients you need to purchase—some might be new to you. Foods that you cannot find in your regular supermarket can often be found in a health food store. If they do not have it in stock they can probably order it for you.

- **If you are allergic** to certain nuts, you can substitute with nuts that you can tolerate or replace them with seeds or grains of various kinds, such as sunflower and pumpkin seeds or hemp seeds.

- **Make sure** you have the utensils you need. (See tips on page 60.)

- **Select** the right program for you.

- **Start preparing** yourself a few weeks in advance by eating more vegetarian food and cutting down on sugar, coffee, nicotine, and alcohol. This will make your transition smoother, and you will likely experience fewer and lighter detox symptoms.

- **If you want to,** tell your friends and family about the program so they can encourage and support you, but remember it is up to you. For some people it may easier not to tell anyone in order to avoid a lot of questions.

- **If you are on medication** or have a serious condition, talk to your doctor or health specialist before you start the program.

- **Try to do the deep breathing exercise,** which can be found in the section on breathing, before you start eating.

- **Regard the meal** as a sacred moment, calm yourself, and send gratitude for the food.

- **Chew your food thoroughly,** as digestion begins in your mouth. Your stomach has no teeth, so food will be more easily digested if you chew properly.

- **It is important not to deny yourself food.** Being hungry for long periods of time is not part of the program. Learn to recognize the difference between cravings and hunger.

- **Do not drink** anything thirty minutes before dinner and for an hour after you finish eating. This will allow the digestive juices to work in peace.

- **Before you come to the end** of your program, sit down for a moment and think about what you can bring with you into your everyday life. Think about the eating habits that you want to maintain and which you can actually do without.

- **On completion of the program,** make sure to ease yourself back into normal eating. Keep raw food as a base and add the food you ate earlier, little by little, so you can really taste it and feel it in your body—almost as if you were eating it for the first time. That will help you understand which foods you were just eating out of habit and which actually taste good and give you energy!

- **Remember** that you are unique—think about what *you* like and what makes you feel good.

- **Prepare your food** with love and enjoy it!

Jeanine Roberts is forty years old, works as a skin care therapist, and lives in Härryda, Sweden with her partner and two children. In her spare time she likes to travel, ride her motorcycle, listen to music, and practice weight lifting as well as running and yoga.

"Dinner on the table in fifteen minutes—it doesn't get any easier than that!"

Good eating habits and taking care of her body have always been important to Jeanine Roberts. And when she was asked if she wanted to try Erica's raw food detox, she didn't hesitate for a moment.

"I was curious about how my body would react, and at the same time I wanted to cleanse and then see what I really needed," she says.

Jeanine has always had issues with her stomach, which was another reason to reboot her system. The goal wasn't to lose weight, but despite that she lost almost ten pounds after twenty-one days on the raw food diet.

"Before I started I was really nervous about how it would affect everyday life, but my partner was out of town when I first started, so I only had myself to think about and that really helped."

In the beginning her thoughts mostly revolved around food, and Jeanine was fixated on the planning of food preparation and how she would have time to eat all the meals. She felt like she ate almost all the time. She absolutely never went hungry, with the exception of one day when she did not like the food that she had prepared.

"There were a couple of recipes that I didn't care for, but I just replaced them with a couple of avocados."

The sugar cravings were gone after a few days and did not return until the end of the program.

"By the third week, something happened. My body was literally screaming for sugar. But I managed to control the cravings by focusing on the fact that I only had a few days left."

Detoxing went well, Jeanine felt very light, and her stomach worked perfectly.

"I felt so refreshed. I slept great and my colleagues took a real interest in what I was doing. I shared some recipes with them, and a couple of my colleagues joined me on the detox for a few days."

Jeanine does not agree with those who say that it's complicated and difficult to prepare raw food.

"Dinner is ready in fifteen minutes—it doesn't get any easier than that! The only drawback in the beginning was purchasing all the ingredients. It seemed like a lot, but divided over the three weeks, I realized it wasn't actually more than I usually buy."

Jeanine is now on a nearly 80 percent raw diet, especially for breakfast and lunch. She also incorporates raw food into dinner parties.

"Several of the recipes work great as a side dish to fish or chicken. Guests may choose for themselves if they just want to stick to raw food or add some meat," says Jeanine.

She would consider doing another detox diet soon, and next time she will do it with her partner.

What I liked the most about the raw detox: "It gave me such a boost of energy and exuberance. I felt clear-headed and I loved trying all the recipes."

Favorite recipe: "I have several favorites, but the spinach soup with avocado has got to be number one. I love the chocolate mousse and the carob balls. I especially like to eat the carob balls on Friday nights as the kids are snacking on popcorn."

Good advice to others who want to try a raw detox: "If it feels too hard, then try to put it in perspective; you are only going to do it three weeks, not for the rest of your life. The detox will allow you to cleanse your body and help you find out what you and your body really want and need."

Good Food Gives Us Energy

For me personally, life is about energy. The more energy I have, the easier I can achieve what I want in life, realize my dreams, and keep a positive mindset. That's why raw food is right for me—I'm getting lots of live enzymes and high vibration foods. It recharges me with new energy and does not slow my digestive system down the way cooked food does. There are so many amazing things in life, and because of that I choose to eat good food that gives me energy to live it.

Our Power Plants

Our cells do everything they can to make all the body's functions run smoothly and efficiently. They take care of nutrition and get rid of the things we do not need. The amount of energy that you have is in direct correlation to how well the cells are doing. In short, you could say that each cell can be regarded as a transmitter and a receiver. Cells maintain constant communication among themselves, but each cell is also a separate living unit. Each cell has its individual vibration frequency, and we can increase or decrease this frequency, depending on the food we choose to eat, the thoughts we have, and our stress levels. Cells can suffer from nutrient and oxygen depletion, and waste products stored in the body can make you sick. By eating raw foods that are high in nutrients, we can help the cells to restore and maintain their natural vibration frequency.

   We have different ways to borrow the energy that we lack. We usually drink coffee and eat sugar and other foods with simple carbohydrates. In the long run, it is not sustainable to borrow energy in this way. It creates an imbalance. I borrow energy myself sometimes, but I make sure to pay it back as soon as I can by drinking green juices and getting more sleep.

Energy: Is It a Calorie?

Rather than counting calories in this program, we'll be thinking about sustaining energy. It's about a total balance each day; some meals may have a higher energy density and others lower. Nuts contain a lot of calories and make some meals more caloric, but the important thing is that the nuts supply the fat and protein that is vital for you to function as effectively as possible. Instead of counting calories, this is how I think: the body needs a certain amount of food each day to function at its best, and it is just as important to eat enough as it is to not eat too much—everything in moderation! And what is right for you can vary from day to day, so the main thing is that you get a feel for what is best for you.

Why Do We Eat?

Food is so much more than just nourishment. Every day we eat and drink to function. But we also eat for other reasons—perhaps because we are happy, sad, stressed, or because we just want to indulge. We eat and eat.

Food as nourishment is an essential part of life. When I talk about food I mean food that fills our cells with vital components. The first thing our cells need is oxygen. We can only survive a few minutes without oxygen. Secondly, our cells need water. We can live up to one week without water. The third thing the cells need is food. And the food should be of high quality, so that it can foster the production of healthy, strong, radiant cells!

When you are stressed and craving something sweet or fatty, stop and breathe, drink a glass of water, and you may well find that you are not at all hungry and the craving is gone. All your cells needed were oxygen and water.

The Foundations of a Healthy Life

A healthy life is a life in harmony where we take care of ourselves in a loving way by eating good food, sleeping, breathing fresh air, drinking plenty of water, creating, and making room for laughter and joy. All these different parts of life need to be in harmony in order for us to live an easier and more joyful life.

Sleep

I often read Bamse for my daughter, Saga, and I'm fascinated by Skalman's food and sleep clock. Imagine if we could listen to our inner clocks and thus get more of a routine when it comes to eating and sleeping—we would have so much more energy! Of course, this works in fiction but not in real life. But we can still do the best we can. Mindlessly watching TV or being on the computer until late at night disturbs our sleep rhythm. It takes discipline to develop good sleep habits. We need to teach our bodies to go to sleep at a certain time and to wake up at another.

   To sleep between ten at night and five in the morning is ideal. During sleep the body is subject to a kind of repair work—the body recovers, your inner organs cleanse you, the brain processes the impressions received during the day, and it all gets a chance to fall into place.

Tip! How to best prepare for sleep: turn off the TV, do not eat heavy meals late at night, take a hot bath and air out the room, do not be on the computer after 9 PM, drink a calming herbal tea, write a few words about your day and what your expectations are for the next day. If you have a hard time falling asleep or usually wake up at night, listen to some relaxing music or a CD with meditations.

Nature

We have a tendency to be more tired during the winter, which is not surprising. We are supposed to perform at the same high rate as the rest of the year even though Nature is settling into rest and recuperation. During summer we take it easy and relax—although that's when we get the most energy from the sun. To live with the seasons is the easiest way to regain your natural balance. If we take the time to be outdoors for at least half an hour a day, preferably at midday during the winter months, we will allow ourselves to see the changes in nature that will enable us to develop a more natural rhythm.

The same applies to body weight; it is no wonder that we have a few extra pounds in the winter. It's cold outside and your body needs to protect itself by adding some extra weight. That makes spring a good time to shed some of those extra pounds from winter. During the summer when we fill up on Vitamin D from the sun, we are more energetic and life feels easy. Many people may have more time to make a lifestyle change during the summer. In the fall our bodies start to prepare themselves for darker days, and we go back to our routines, which can be a great opportunity to introduce new habits.

Holistically speaking, we are meant to follow the course of nature, and that's why natural health teaching suggests detoxing around the autumn and spring equinox. In this way we help the body to keep up with the turn of the seasons. But do not let this stop you from doing a detox during other times of year that might suit you better.

Activity

We need to move our bodies in order for them to work optimally—for our hearts to beat and for our lymphatic system to function.

The body needs exercise and movement throughout the day. You can do simple things like taking the stairs instead of the elevator, and biking or walking instead of taking the bus or car. It's better to do a little bit every day than two big workouts a week. Our bodies are meant to stay active and not to be idle. Be active in a way that makes you happy! Keep in mind that overdoing it acidifies your body, and that you need rest and recuperation after you have exercised.

Respiration

By breathing you fill your cells with oxygen. The more oxygen your cells have, the better chance you have of staying healthy. Breathing is one of the methods we use to clean ourselves. When you eat something that is not good for you, you get bad breath.

Here's a simple deep breathing exercise: Breathe out, and then really squeeze out all the oxygen you have in your lungs. Count to four while you breathe in. Hold your breath, while you count to sixteen. Release your breath while you count to eight. Repeat the exercise ten times. Do this while standing up, holding your palms against your chest and stomach and feel how your breath fills your chest and even in your stomach. This exercise is great to do at the beginning of the day and also just before eating. You have filled your cells with oxygen—which is their greatest need.

Practicing Meditation and Being More Present

To be more present in the moment, you can use time-tested methods such as meditation, yoga, qigong, or tai chi. In practicing being more present, you become "one" with what is happening, and you can practice even when you eat. Carefully consider each bite, and feel the flavors explode in your mouth.

To meditate is not as difficult as it may sound if you haven't tried it before. It's simply about being present here and now. It can be as simple as being still for a moment, wherever you may be, and maybe close your eyes and focus entirely on yourself and your own energy. Meditation is not all about assuming the lotus position with your eyes closed for hours—you can also practice meditation while standing, walking, jumping, running, or playing. The main thing is that you are "present" in the here and now.

Make an investment in yourself and practice short meditations as soon as you get the opportunity. Turn your energy inward and direct love and gratitude to yourself. Or turn your energy outward; watch how the leaves move in the wind, how they sound, and what they smell like.

There are a lot of books on meditation—in the inspiration list, there are a few titles that I have found valuable.

Tip: A quiet moment each day can remind you of the motivation you have to follow through with the program. Try to return to that feeling when you feel like you want to give up and quit the program.

Relationships

The most important relationship you have is the relationship with yourself. You are the person that you will always live with, day and night, twenty-four hours a day. So get to know yourself: What do you like? What makes you feel good? What makes you happy in life?

When it comes to our own performance, most of us have two inner voices that compete for space—the cheerleader and the judge. Often, one is stronger

than the other. For example, try to recognize it and let your cheerleader come out.

Take off your self-critical glasses and try to take a less judgmental look at yourself. How does it feel not to be judged by yourself or others? When your relationship with yourself is free from perceptions and criticism you will see other relationships in a different light. It will make it easier to understand what you have to learn from the people you meet, and what relationships are good for you and which ones are not.

It is easier to implement a lifestyle change if you surround yourself with people who support you and see the good in what you do for yourself. Sometimes we meet people who are reluctant to change their own lives and project that negative fear of change on others. Do not let other people's restrictions limit you.

Organic Food

Choosing organic food is part of a healthy life because it benefits fellow human beings and the well-being of our planet. With organic ingredients, we give the body the best possible nutrition. We also help the world's ecosystems function as well as possible.

When we choose organic, we refrain from pesticides, additives, artificial flavoring, refined foods, and chemicals that pollute not only our bodies but also our fellow human beings and our planet.

Sure, organic food is often more expensive, but think of the price you could pay. It's not just your own health but the health of our whole earth that's at stake. Be more attentive to what you put into your shopping cart and where your money goes. Make an investment in yourself!

Choose organic to the extent that you are comfortable with, and select your other food with happy and grateful thoughts.

Food Combinations and Acid–Alkaline Balance

Food Combinations

Within the raw food movement, there are various theories about how to get even more energy. One of these theories is combining foods based on how our bodies metabolize them. By combining various foods that we digest slowly or quickly, we will get more bloated and have a sense of "rot" of the intestines. In combining the wrong foods we may also deplete energy. The digestive system is one of the systems in the body that requires the most energy. By eating a combination of foods that require different amounts of time to digest, we may find that the food makes us tired and lethargic.

A few tips!

- Eat melon by itself since it only takes fifteen minutes to break down in the stomach.
- Do not mix carbohydrates with protein.
- Green leafy vegetables can be combined without restrictions.
- Fruit should only be eaten on an empty stomach or at least three hours after a meal.
- Fruit has the shortest digestion span and can cause an upset stomach when combined with other foods.
- Select one type of fat—either oil, avocados, nuts or seeds—per meal.

I encourage you to see what works for you and your body! Some people can combine freely and not experience the slightest discomfort, while people with a sensitive stomach—like me—know immediately when there's too much going on for my digestive system to work well, and then have to reconsider their eating habits and eliminate what doesn't work.

The recipes in this book do not all follow the correct food combinations since I feel that if you are too strict it's very easy to become bored with raw food. If raw food stops being fun, I may pick a cinnamon bun over a raw food pie. And a raw food pie, even without the right food combinations, is a much better option!

Acid–Alkaline Balance

In short, you could say that fruits and vegetables are alkaline forming. There are five main factors affecting both the acid and the alkaline balances: genes, food, climate, digestive function, and stress. You can be acidic because of stress, anger, incorrect diet, excessive exercise, or other factors that have a negative effect on your life. The general recommendation is that you eat 70 to 80 percent alkaline-forming foods and 20 to 30 percent acid-forming foods. The pH of the saliva should be at 7.0 to 7.8, and the ideal pH value in the blood is 7.365. Your body works constantly to maintain this value in the blood. Only a small adjustment in any direction could have health consequences. If you are over-acidic, you reduce the absorption of oxygen to the cells, thus impairing your metabolism and cell production.

You can test your pH with a test strip that you buy at the pharmacy. Check your value every morning for a week just before you eat a meal, keep track of your results, and calculate an average for the week.

Tips on acid/alkaline foods:

- Lemon, which is really acidic by itself, is actually alkaline forming. That's why you start the day with a glass of water with lemon during the program—to start your day alkaline.

- Acid-forming foods are milk and milk products, animal products, and grain. Particularly acid forming are coffee, black tea, soft drinks, sweets, and alcohol.

- A daily intake of leafy greens helps the body become more alkaline. Chlorophyll is what makes the leaves green, which I think of as concentrated sunshine. Chlorophyll resembles the hemoglobin in blood—what makes them different from each other is that chlorophyll contains magnesium, while hemoglobin contains iron. So the more leafy greens that we eat, the easier it is to purify our blood. And the purer the blood, the healthier we are.

• Signs that you are acidic can include: joint pain, fatigue, sleeping difficulties, skin rashes, and more.

You can eat great and healthy foods that are alkaline forming and still continue to be acidic. If you are in a foul mood and not enjoying your food, that will also make you acidic. In other words, you can help your body become more alkaline by being happier, getting more rest, getting moderate exercise, and eating good food.

If you are interested in reading more about food combinations and acid–alkaline balance, you will find suggestions in the back of the book under "Inspiration and Further Reading."

What is Detox?

Detox is short for detoxification, and in short, it is cleansing the intestines as well as the internal organs by a change of diet.

Our bodies naturally detox every day. The body has its own cleaning system that works constantly—by urine, feces, sweat, and with our breath, we constantly detoxify. Sometimes we eat fewer healthy foods or eat more than our bodies can handle. Detoxing is about taking in just as much as we can use up.

We take in toxins from pollution, chemicals, and food additives, but also by medicine and tobacco. But the worst pollution is self-inflicted by eating junk food or food combinations that are not good for us. The food remains undigested in the intestine, which causes it to putrefy, allowing toxins to spread into the blood stream through the intestinal wall. It encumbers the kidneys and liver, whose job it is to detoxify us and clean out these substances. It is often said that 70 percent of the immune system sits in the stomach. In order to stay as healthy as possible, it is therefore critical to have properly functioning bowels.

When bowels and internal organs become congested, various imbalances occur in the body, and you may feel depleted, tired, have sore joints, and suffer from insomnia. In many cases, nutritional therapists recommend first doing a detox before determining a diagnosis, just to make it easier to see what the real problem is.

The detox programs that appear in newspapers and magazines vary, but usually exclude animal products, gluten, dairy, and sugar. Even coffee and alcohol are traditionally excluded during a detox.

What happens during and after a detox varies from person to person, depending on how you have lived before. For example, you might experience detox symptoms such as headaches and fatigue. If the symptoms are too strong, you need to ease yourself into it so the body does not detoxify too quickly.

Most people notice pretty quickly that they feel more alert, have smoother skin, have less indigestion, feel better in their joints, and that their eyes take on a different glow and that happiness and peace spread throughout their systems.

You can help the body detox by drinking good quality water and dry brushing your skin—the skin is the largest cleansing organ we have. If you are having problems with your skin, it may be a result of what you eat and how your stomach and gut feel. Get moderate excercise. Rest when needed. Cut down on stress and obligations.

Detox powders and solids
The detox powders that are available at health food stores are formulated to support your body's various phases of purging and help your body cleanse itself. A detox powder is a convenient way to clean out and can also initiate a lifestyle change. It's better than doing nothing at all, but remember that there is a good reason for making a change for better and healthier habits, which can function long term in everyday life.

Fasting means that you only drink liquids during a set number of days. For example, when drinking fresh juices, you do so to put the least strain on your body and digestion. But you have to remember that there are poisons in our fat and if we lose weight too fast, they can be released because they are fat-soluble. Weight loss that is too rapid can cause the toxins to release into the blood stream. Sometimes it may be better to go for slower, more sustainable weight loss where the toxins are being cleaned out of the body more gently.

Maria Olovson is thirty years old and lives in a house outside Umeå, Sweden with her partner. She works in an office and is generally very interested in health, practices yoga at home, and takes hikes through the mountains.

"I felt more energetic after just a few days."

For a long time, Maria Olovson felt that there was something missing. She couldn't put her finger on it, but she suspected it had to do with her eating habits. When Erica Palmcrantz Aziz gave a lecture in the neighboring town, Maria went and listened to it, and the pieces started falling into place. She discovered that what Erica was talking about was consistent with her own desire to break bad habits. Maria decided to use raw food to do a proper cleanse, and she contacted Erica to ask for some ideas on how to get started.

"I needed guidance on how to think, so Erica asked if I wanted to try her detox program," says Maria. Maria did the twenty-one-day program, except for a little cheating towards the end. It was during Easter and the family was having a big Easter celebration that Maria could not resist. Altogether, it was nineteen days of detox.

"It was one of the most difficult but best things I've ever done! The first week I was very cold. I was cold all the time, but the desire and the motivation was so strong that I didn't consider quitting."

But Maria ran into another trial when she had to go on a business trip.

"I simply had to bring my own food. Sure, it took some planning, but it worked," she says.

Already after a few days she felt that "toxins" such as sugar, caffeine, and gluten left the body, and, although she was careless with snacks, her body was filled with lots of energy.

"I probably would have felt even more energized if I ate everything I was supposed to. Now, I have learned to listen to my body and I realize how important it is to eat what I actually should, and at set times."

The first week was drawing to an end, and Maria was in high spirits. Her unwitting colleagues marveled at her ambition.

"I chose not to tell many people what I was doing. I did not want a lot of questions from people. I wanted it to be my special thing. But at the beginning of the second week, it was like pulling the plug—my motivation went down and everything tasted disgusting."

"I felt like a small cow, I ate and ate and the food never left my mouth. Occasionally, the old habits threatened to sneak back in."

But Maria had her tricks to outwit her cravings. At times she ate more nuts and seeds than she should have, and a couple of times she went off the daily menu.

"Instead of following the daily menu to the letter, I chose dishes that felt right for me that day."

For Maria Olovson, the detox became not only a physical purification, but also a way to analyze why she had adopted some habits and why she had chosen certain paths in life. It was also a test to see how she would manage without sugar.

"I'm like a magnet for sugar, I put it in my mouth without thinking. Now, instead of candy or cake, I eat berries or a raw bar."

Maria has also introduced elements of raw food to her regular diet, especially for breakfast and lunch. Soon she will partake in a shorter raw detox.

"This time, I will explore other raw food recipes because I think a raw diet, however it's done, makes your body and soul harmonious."

What I liked the most about the raw detox: "That I have rediscovered myself. When you eat completely clean foods, a lot happens in both body and soul. Now I see more clearly why I make certain choices in life!"

Favorite recipes: "The sushi rolls and the avocado and cucumber soups. The soups are my absolute favorite. The first time I ate one of the soups I didn't think it would fill me up, but it really did . . ."

Good advice to others who want to try the raw detox: "Drink, drink, drink! A hydrated body is divine. Learn more about raw food before you detox and remember that everything depends on your will power—it's all about putting your mind to it."

Being Regular

Keeping your bowels regular is necessary. The foods that we eat in the Western world today do not excercise the intestines as they should.

  This is actually a big problem for many. They don't eliminate often enough. We can have nearly six pounds of undigested food in our intestines waiting to be eliminated. If you don't go to the bathroom often enough, you will have a lot of gas, and the undigested food will cause toxins to seep into the bloodstream. When intestines work well you will eliminate once or twice a day. When you eat more fiber than you're used to your stomach may react by getting constipated. In that case, it is important that you empty your bowel. Or you may have to go to the toilet a few extra times.

Tips on how to make your stomach more regular:

- Take 2 tablespoons crushed psyllium husk and mix into a glass of water. Stir and drink. Remember to drink water throughout the day to keep yourself regular.

- Chia seeds mixed with water help the stomach get going since they are rich in dietary fiber. They form a gel when soaked.

- Soak flax seeds in water overnight and drink first thing in the morning. Strain flax seeds first or drink as it is.

- You can also do a colon cleansing. At the pharmacy you can buy an enema that you can use at home. Or go to an authorized colon-cleansing specialist and do a more thorough colon cleansing.

Is Body Weight Important?

Scientific studies worldwide indicate that with weight loss diets people regain the lost weight plus some after dieting. When you have a lifestyle change that fits into your daily life and that gives you pleasure and joy, it will be easier to maintain your weight after weight loss and will give you a better chance to find your natural weight.

Weight: Normal, Over, or Under?
For people with excess weight I hope to convey a new thinking about food that can lead to weight loss that will last a lifetime, rather than a quick but short-term solution. The problem for many who are overweight is often a tendency to try many different diets which creates a yo-yo effect between gaining and losing weight without finding a balance. One's natural weight is only maintained for a short while.

  If you are underweight, your problem tends to be ignored even though it can feel just as difficult to be underweight as it is to be overweight. If you are underweight, it may be because the body cannot absorb the nutrients you eat, or you don't eat enough. With the help of raw food, you can deal with that kind of imbalance and you may even gain weight.

  If you are already at your ideal weight and don't want to lose anything, just eat until you feel comfortably full. You may still lose some weight as you are cleansing. You will gain those pounds back, but with the help of nutritious food.

Natural Weight

People who I have coached over a period time who wanted to lose weight have in fact often found that they lose their weight obsession when they eat raw food. When the body receives food that brings joy, strength, and inner beauty it will result in a natural and lasting weight loss. My mother, Bitte, who you may remember from my book *Raw Food: A Complete Guide for Every Meal of the Day*, lost 33 pounds in her first year with raw food, and she says she's never eaten so well or so much. She had not even focused on losing weight, but just wanted to try and see what raw food was all about. After five years with mostly raw food in her diet, she has now lost another ten pounds, and she has never felt as young and beautiful in body as well as mind. Her body has stabilized at its natural weight.

You Decide

You have to decide for yourself what the right weight for you is. To find your ideal weight, you need to stop comparing yourself to others and instead find the weight that makes you comfortable, gives you a high energy level, and makes you feel good about yourself. Whether you want to lose or gain weight, remember that everything is a process and everything has to take its own time. Encourage yourself as you would with your best friend—things won't be easier if you get down on yourself. Cheer up!

Quizzes: Reflections to Take to Heart

When we change the way we eat we might question our food. One way to visualize and reflect on these questions may be to write them down. To help you with that, you can use this quiz, which consists of questions that give you an opportunity to reflect on your own experiences. It can also be a great help to return to your reflections later to see how you have changed with time.

Daily Questions and Reflections

There are three questions you can answer every day to help you better monitor how you feel. The other questions you can answer before, during, or after the program. Save your answers and get them out next time you do the program and see what has changed since last time.

Daily Checklist

- How was your energy level today? How was the overall balance: have you slept well, were you active enough, did you remember to drink water, did you go out for some fresh air?

- In what situations have you wanted to eat something other than what is in the program? And why do you think that was?

- Reflect on the day and what experiences you have had. How do you feel about yourself today? Do you feel better about yourself or worse?

End your day by writing down three things that were good and that make you proud of yourself.

How do you feel about food?

- There are many reasons why food doesn't satisfy us. It may be that we forget to breathe or drink water. Sometimes it may simply be that we are not eating enough and need to increase the size of our meals. So check to see if you are satisfied after eating. If not, consider why. Do you think it was a need other than food that needs to be fulfilled?

- Have you noticed any difference between what it was like when you ate "normal" food and how it feels since you started with raw food?

- When are you really hungry? Do you eat only when you are hungry? A lot of times we eat for other reasons. Learn how to identify when you are hungry "for real" and when you eat for some other reason.

Changed Habits
- If you are looking to quit the program, what is the reason for that? If you considered ending the program but did not, what was it that made you continue? Write down the reasons why you chose to quit/continue.

- What are your diet and life like when everything is as you want it to be? Why is it that you don't eat or live that way now? Does it have to do with limitations that you set up? How do you feel now? How do you think you would feel if you implemented these changes?

Examining your relationship with food and its effects on the body and mood is a bit like finding "tools" that work. You have your own nuts that need special wrenches, but if you do not know that there are wrenches, you don't even know that it is possible to unscrew the nuts. So see what kind of bolts, nails, and screws you have, and which tools are right for you—put them in your toolbox and take them out when it's necessary to screw and hammer here and there.

Time to Start!

One day, three days, a week, or three weeks—regardless of the length of the program you have chosen, you now have a fantastic opportunity to change your lifestyle and become more harmonious.

Life is all about energy. Good food gives us energy, but if we eat food that, on the contrary, takes energy away from us, then we are not able to live life fully. If we choose food that gives the body and mind optimum nutrition and maximum energy, our lives improve.

With curiosity and an open mind you will have an exciting time ahead of you!

Planning Ahead and New Routines

Preparing raw food may seem a little complicated the first week, but once you get into the habit of taking the food processor out, it is easy. In the beginning, you may want to set aside time for cooking. It does require, for example, some preparation the night before if you want to bring your own lunch to work. If you're in a bind, you can run into a grocery store at lunch, get some leafy greens and vegetables, some seeds and nuts, and there's your lunch salad! It usually just takes a week before you find out how quick and easy it is to prepare raw food as opposed to "regular food."

It's a good idea to start preparing food before you get really hungry. When we are really hungry our blood sugar levels decrease, which may put you in a bad mood and make you lose your patience.

The Program

I have simplified the program by repeating the same breakfast several days. Weekend breakfasts are a little different to make them special. If you prefer to eat the same breakfast for the entire program, then that's fine, too.

Every day there is a new recipe for snacks and dinner. If you prefer, you can prepare these meals in advance. One idea is to make two servings and save one for the following day. As an example, you can change the program around to eat the same snacks/dinner two days in a row. Then, use those recipes on another day. Don't worry about following the program too strictly—it's more important to make sure that you can fit it into your everyday life.

The recipes range from Monday to Sunday to follow the week. But you can also start on a Friday and have the weekend to start your change.

Servings

Each recipe states how many servings it makes. The recipes are made for women with average activity levels. Figure out how much food you need to get enough energy and adjust the amount, so that you do not go around hungry. Remember that having a craving and being hungry are two different things. Try to distinguish between the two.

Regular Meals

Try to eat at about the same time each day. Over the weekend it will differ a little if you like to sleep a little longer. It is important to have meals at regular times to keep a balanced blood sugar level and to allow the digestive system to rest between meals. If you have a craving for something, you can chew a licorice root, some fennel seeds, or drink herbal tea or ginger water.

TIP: Take out your ingredients about 30 minutes before eating so that they reach room temperature.

Good Advice along the Way

Daily Ideas

- Remember to drink water. But make sure not to drink anything half an hour before and one hour after you eat lunch and dinner. If you want to rinse your mouth after you eat, then that is okay.

- Fennel seed is a substitute for chewing gum after meals. Eating fennel seeds helps your digestion and freshens your mouth.

- If you crave sweets, chew a piece of a licorice root.

- If you feel unusually cold, it is because the body is detoxifying itself. To get your internal temperature up, you can drink ginger water with lemon or herbal tea. Put on warm clothes, take a warm shower, or move around.

- Remember to power down before you eat and take a few conscious breaths. Eat in peace and quiet. Focus on your food and focus on the energy that you bring your body. Chew thoroughly. Talk about fun things.

- Try to buy organic as much as you can. Otherwise, do your best to choose what's been grown locally.

- Make your own juices. Another, less beneficial option, is to buy bottled fresh juices.

- Try to make your workout low intensity and do stretching exercises to help the body to cleanse itself. If you feel that you have lots of energy, you can do some medium-impact exercise.

- Each morning, try to pay attention to how your body feels. Before going to bed, thank your body for the day that has passed.

- Allow yourself to rest. The body sends you signals that are important to listen to.

- Enjoy and season your food with the best spice—love!

Water

When we are born we are made up of about 90 percent water; as adults, we should have about 70 percent of water in our bodies to be healthy. In the book *Your Body's Many Cries for Water*, Dr. Fereydoon Batmanghelidj describes how our mental acuity and brain efficiency are adversely affected by dehydration, and he also thinks that a good fluid balance in the body can make us feel better and feel happier.

The best way to take in fluids is to eat a diet that is 70 percent water. When water is added in combination with vitamins and minerals, the body has an easier time absorbing them. But it is important that the water we drink is clean. There are various water purifiers that remove chemicals, chlorine, and other things that can degrade its quality. If you live near a natural source, go there and get fresh spring water, which is the water that has the very best quality.

Water transports nutrients to our cells and makes sure that they stay healthy, but it also has an important function in the removal of waste. We pee, breathe, and sweat out water. As you eat more and more raw food, you will feel that your sweat does not smell as much. It's because you're eating clean food and the body does not carry as much waste.

Coffee or Tea

If you're used to drinking coffee or tea several times a day, you can exchange that during the program for yerba mate, an herb from South America that has been used since ancient times. This drink will perk you up and intensifies the cleansing process. Yerba mate can also make you less hungry, as it contains a natural form of caffeine (for advice on how to prepare it, see page 64).

Nicotine, Medicine, and Supplements

I have a close friend who actually used a detox program to quit smoking. When the body receives pure food it reduces the craving for nicotine. It is recommended to avoid nicotine during the program, but remember that it is better to make a long-term lifestyle change and get rid of the nicotine at your own pace.

I strongly encourage you to refrain from medication during the program. Consult with your doctor before making any medical decisions.

If you usually take supplements, decide for yourself if you want to take a break during the program or if you want to continue. If you are in the middle of a regimen recommended by a natural healer, consult him or her and see what advice you get.

If you live far from the equator, D vitamins are fine to take during the darker periods of the year, as the winter sun does not provide enough.

Kitchen Tools You Need

- A cutting board, preferably made of wood

- A good knife

- A food processor to make foods like pie crusts and nut and seed mixtures. A small food processor is handy if you want to make smaller batches.

- A blender for smoothies, dressings, and sauces. You could also use an immersion blender, but a regular blender will make the food creamier and smoother.

- A nut milk bag or a fine mesh strainer to make nut milk of various types. Once you get used to making nut milks, it takes about five minutes, but expect it to take a few more minutes until you get the hang of it.

- A citrus press, to squeeze your own lemon juice.

- A juice extractor to juice carrots, beets, apples, and so forth. There are juicers of various brands, types, and price ranges available. See what works for your kitchen and your wallet.

- A dehydrator is a kind of "raw food oven" that you can set to 107 F (42 C) degrees, and they are often equipped with a timer. They are convenient if you want to "cook" when you're at work or bake bread overnight. If you do not have a dehydrator, you can use your regular oven. Set it to 107 F (42 C) degrees, or as close as you can get. Keep the door slightly open to let out the steam, or air it out occasionally. The drying time may differ depending on whether you use a dehydrator or a conventional oven. Experiment to find how long you need to bake foods in your oven. When using the dehydrator, you need something called teflex, which is waxed baking paper. If you use a regular oven, use parchment paper-like sheets made of silicone, which you can buy at any good kitchen store.

Soaking – How To

- Dry nuts and seeds contain a so-called inhibitor, which is like an enzyme that keeps the seed dormant. When the nuts and the seeds get wet the enzyme is released and makes the nutrient content increase, and they become more easily digestible.

- The recipes indicate the dry amount to soak. During soaking, the food will increase in volume.

- Soaking times given are only a recommendation, so try and see what works best. Every day you will have a list of what you need to prepare and approximately how long it will take. Sometimes it's better to soak for one hour than not at all. If you find that soaking is too complicated, then you can opt out of it. But in that case, you have to be aware of your stomach so that you don't become too bloated—when you don't soak your nuts and seeds they are harder to digest.

- Use plenty of water when you soak buckwheat, nuts, and seeds. And discard the soaking water, even when you soak sprouts. Various nuts and seeds need different lengths of soaking time, so see each separate recipe for the recommended time.

- When you soak dried fruit, pour the water so that it is a little more than an inch (three cm) above the dried fruit and place in the fridge. The soaking water can then be used instead of tap water for smoothies and dressings, or when baking. The soaked fruit can be stored one to two days in a tightly sealed jar in the fridge.

    Fresh dates are those that have a pit inside and do not need to be soaked. The dried, pitted ones may need to be soaked, depending on how dry they are.

- Sun-dried tomatoes (those that are not in oil) require about one hour to soften. You can store the soaked sun-dried tomatoes in the fridge for a few days.

Sprouting

If you have a habit of sprouting, you may continue to do so during the program. If you are a beginner, think about whether you want to bring this process into your life as well. If not, you can wait and start sprouting when you become a more experienced raw food cook.

How Long Will It Keep?

- Dressing keeps for two days.

- Nut or seed mixtures/dipping sauce will keep for two to three days in a tightly sealed jar.

- Snacks and raw food bars will keep for about a week in the refrigerator and several months in the freezer.

- Dried crackers, cakes, and pizza crusts will also keep for several months. The drier they are, the longer they will keep. Store in a tightly sealed jar at room or pantry temperature. If you make softer cakes, you can store them in the fridge for about a week.

A Typical Day

These are just suggested times, adjusting the meals to the times that fit you. Just make sure not to let more than three hours pass between meals, and eat at about the same time each day.

Breakfast (7-9 AM)
Start your day with a glass of lukewarm water with lemon juice. If you are used to drinking coffee in the morning, drink a cup of yerba mate (see page 71) before breakfast, and you will get the boost that you're used to. Brew it the same way you would tea, or soak it overnight and make it as a real raw food tea. To soak, do the following: Take 1 tablespoon of the herb and put into a cup of purified water over night. In the morning, strain it and add about 1½-1¾ cup (300-400 ml) lukewarm water. If you can, wait for about 30 minutes after you have been drinking water and yerba mate before you eat your breakfast.

The breakfast will help you to restore fluid balance after sleep and clear the intestines. Breakfasts consist of fruits and vegetables. By mixing the fruit with celery, fennel, and zucchini we add some green to the morning meal.

Blending the fruit will make digesting it easier, and the fiber will help to keep things moving. Blended drinks also fill you up more than juice.

If you tend to be hungry in the morning, you can top your fruit cereal with buckwheat, chia seeds, hemp seeds, pumpkin, or sunflower seeds that have been soaked. I recommend avoiding seeds, grains, and buckwheat during the second week, when we focus more on cleansing.

If you want to add superfoods like açai powder, nettle powder, or rosehip flour for your breakfast, you should and it will provide extra strength.

Snacks in the Late Morning

Choose fruits and vegetables such as avocado, carrots, cucumbers, lettuce, cabbage, apples, berries of various kinds, or pears.

Lunch (11:30-12:30)

Large salad with your choice of ingredients. Serve with a dressing and avocado or onion crackers. Eat until you are comfortably full.

Snack (3-4 PM)

Here's your chance to eat something yummy. Nuts, seeds, and dried fruit help you avoid the mid-afternoon slump, and will also take care of any sugar cravings. During week 2, which focuses on cleansing, snack time will be mostly fruits and vegetables.

Dinner (6-8 PM)

Try to eat no later than three hours before bedtime, so that your digestive system gets a rest. If you crave something at night, drink water, herbal teas/ginger water, and breathe. Prepare for the next day, both practically and mentally. Go over the quiz questions and write in your journal.

The best spice is love!

Raw Food Ingredients

Raw food diets sometimes include honey, agave nectar, and cocoa. In this book, these have been substituted by soaked dried fruit. Cocoa is replaced with carob powder, which has a similar taste but no caffeine.

  Superfoods are, in short, foods that are particularly packed with nutrients. Many berries, powders, and seeds are superfoods.

Açai are berries that grow on palm trees in the Amazon and are incredibly rich in antioxidants. The taste is a mixture of cocoa, olives, and raisins. Use for breakfasts and smoothies.

Buckwheat is an herb and therefore gluten-free. Buckwheat needs to be soaked for about eight hours. During soaking a reddish slime is formed that you need to rinse off carefully. You can sprout buckwheat in one to three days in order to optimize the nutrition. Buckwheat is particularly rich in the minerals magnesium, zinc, and iron.

Carob powder tastes a lot like cocoa and comes from the carob tree that grows around the Mediterranean. Carob is rich in iron and calcium and, unlike cocoa, contains no caffeine.

Chia seeds are rich in dietary fiber, protein, antioxidants, omega-3 fatty acids, and minerals and amino acids. When chia seeds are soaked, they absorb water up to twelve times their own weight. The seeds act as a blood glucose stabilizer. They have a neutral taste and are eaten soaked, as cereal, mixed into a fruit cereal, or used in smoothies. The small seeds are usually my rescue when I feel hunger setting in—I stir some in a glass of lukewarm tea, wait ten minutes, and drink. My blood sugar stabilizes, and I get an easy and comfortable sensation of being full. It's best to soak them a little longer, about four to eight hours.

Cocoa nibs come from the raw cocoa bean. Cocoa bean is one of the best natural sources of magnesium, iron, and chromium and is also incredibly rich in antioxidants. Remember that cocoa can make you really perky, so take it easy in the evening with those little yummies. The pieces are delicious to use in smoothies, sprinkle on top of raw ice cream, or just nibble on as they are with goji berries.

Cocoa butter is a cold-pressed product of the cocoa bean. The cocoa butter is rich in vitamin E and beneficial fatty acids. With cocoa butter you can make raw truffles. Cocoa butter is also soft and smooth to use on the skin. In order to use it, you must first melt it slowly over a lukewarm double boiler.

Coconut oil contains saturated fat, but it is a saturated fat that the body needs and that helps the metabolism. The oil is liquid at about 75 F (25 C) degrees. If the oil is solid, liquefy it over a lukewarm double boiler. Coconut oil also contains lauric acid and caprylic acid, which have an antibacterial affect on the body. When I get a little sweet craving I take a teaspoon of coconut oil—and that takes care of it. The oil is also ideal for moisturizing your skin.

Goji berries are a red berry that is both sweet and sour. Goji berries have long been used in oriental medicine to promote strength and longevity. The berries contain a large amount of vitamin C, beta-carotene, amino acids, and minerals and trace elements.

Ground vanilla bean has a wonderful flavor. I use ground vanilla bean for my breakfasts, smoothies, truffles, and snack balls—it always enhances the flavor.

Hemp seeds are small, soft seeds that have a smooth, nutty flavor. They are rich in essential fatty acids and amino acids. Hemp seeds are great to sprinkle on a salad or breakfast, or to mix into a milk.

Licorice helps to fight sweet cravings and stabilizes blood sugar. I always have a root in my pocket to chew on when I need it.

Lucuma is a fruit that is dried and ground into a powder. Lucuma has a mild, mellow flavor of caramel and vanilla. It's great as a sweetener because it has a low glycemic index and is rich in iron and beta carotene. I use lucuma in smoothies, raw ice cream, and the best raw food goodies.

Mesquite is a powder that originally comes from an oblong bean pod. It naturally contains a little fructose, gives a rich, smoky, and caramel-like flavor, and is excellent in desserts and smoothies. It has a high fiber content and is rich in calcium, iron, magnesium, and zinc. It is delicious mixed with carob and lucuma powder for treats and smoothies.

Mulberries (white) are sweet, with a flavor reminiscent of caramel. Mulberry has the ability to stabilize blood sugar levels and raise good cholesterol. Mulberry contains vitamin C, vitamin K, iron, and calcium. Eat them on their own or use them to treat yourself in breakfasts and smoothies.

Nettle powder is a superfood common in Sweden that is rich in chlorophyll; vitamins A, C, and D; iron; and calcium. You can sprinkle nettle powder on your breakfast or green smoothies and energy soups. Nettle tea works as a cleanser for the body and is recommended during the program.

Rosehip powder is rosehips that are dried after harvest and ground finely. The orange color is evidence that the rose hips are rich in beta-carotene, which is a precursor to vitamin A. It is also rich in many other antioxidants.

Sauerkraut and other lacto-fermented vegetables are fermented foods that are good for digestion and provide the body with enzymes. Sauerkraut is fermented by bacteria (lactobacilli) that settle in the intestines and produce beneficial lactic acid and vitamins, especially B vitamins.

Seaweed comes in several forms. Arame is the algae that is mildest in taste. Wakame, hiziki, and dulse are examples of other algae. Unroasted nori sheets are used every week in the program and have a mild seaweed flavor. Seaweed is a good source of protein and contains trace elements and minerals. It also aids in bringing heavy metals out of the body.

Sesame seeds (unhulled) are rich in minerals and unsaturated fats—they're especially rich in calcium and iron. You can make your own sesame milk and raw tahini of unhulled sesame seeds.

Shoots are seeds that are sprouted and have been allowed to grow. To get shoots you need soil, unless you are using a special sprouter. After sowing, it takes about ten to twelve days before you can harvest them. Shoots are amazingly nutritious, and the green of the shoots is from chlorophyll, which helps to purify our blood. The most common shoots are sunflower shoots and pea shoots, which can be found in many supermarkets.

Spirulina is a freshwater algae high in protein, vitamin B12, and chlorophyll. Spirulina strengthens the immune system, helps to balance blood sugar, and gives an energy boost. I often begin and end my days with spirulina, lime juice, a pinch of Himalayan salt, and water—a perfect mini-breakfast or mini-supper.

Sprouts, such as green lentil sprouts, alfalfa sprouts, and mung bean sprouts, are easily sprouted at home. You can also sprout radish and broccoli seeds, which are very flavorful.

Scientists believe that sprouts' antioxidant effect is ten times higher than the fully grown plant. If the sprouts are allowed to develop shoots and are exposed to sunlight, they become greener and you get a fresh source of chlorophyll, which is known to have cleansing, anti-inflammatory, and rejuvenating properties.

Stevia is an herb that does not affect blood sugar and contains no calories but that is about a hundred times sweeter than sugar. Stevia is available as dried leaves, green or white powder, and liquid. It is easy to overdo it with stevia, start with very little and taste.

Tamari is a non pasteurized, fermented soy sauce used to provide saltiness in a dish. It works well in dressings and to drizzle over a salad.

Wasabi is available as a powder or as a paste and has a flavor that resembles horseradish. It's used in raw sushi rolls and dipping sauce. The wasabi paste is not 100 percent raw but is still used to make raw food sushi resemble regular sushi.
It takes very little to give plenty of flavor.

Yacon syrup is a sweetener with a low GI that is extracted from the yacon root. The flavor is reminiscent of rich maple syrup. Yacon syrup is rich in antioxidants and potassium and acts as a prebiotic for the intestine (it helps create a healthy culture of bacteria in the stomach).

Yerba mate is an herb with less caffeine than coffee or tea and more theophylline and theobromine. Theophylline dilates the bronchial tubes and facilitates oxygenation. Theobromine stimulates the heart and acts like a minor muscle relaxant and diuretic. Yerba mate has long been used in South America for its invigorating effect.

One-Day Menu—Instant Purification!

This one-day program is ideal if you want to do a quick cleanse or if you are a beginner. The good thing is that you will actually notice a difference after just one day.

When we prepare the food in the blender, as we will do a lot during this one-day menu, we preserve a lot of the fibers. This gives your stomach a workout without making it too tough on your digestive system, since the food is already broken down when it reaches the stomach. Still, remember to chew your smoothie and soup. When you chew, you break down the food even more and you use your jaw muscles.

BREAKFAST
Apple cereal
1 serving
Celery is great in the morning! Mixed with pear and apple, it gives you a good sweet and sour start to the day.

1 apple
1 pear
2 sticks celery
1 tablespoon water
optional: cinnamon

Cut the apple, pear, and celery into pieces and put in a blender. Blend fruit and vegetables with water to a smooth consistency. Spice it up with cinnamon if you like.

SNACK
Blue-green smoothie
1 serving
Add a piece of ginger for more flavor and to boost your immune system!

½ pear
½ cup (100 ml) blueberries
1½ ounce (40 g) spinach
1½-2 cups (300-500 ml) water
½ avocado

Cut the pear into pieces. Mix pears, blueberries, spinach, and water thoroughly in blender. Add water in small amounts. Add avocado and blend again. Taste and check to see if you want to add more water.

LUNCH & DINNER **Spinach soup**

Serves 2

This soup is best if prepared just before eating, but for practical reasons, this recipe is enough for both lunch and dinner to save you a little preparation time. Pour the dinner portion in a tightly sealed container, preferably a glass jar. You may want to make only half the recipe if you are cooking for lunch on one occasion and dinner at another.

4 inches (10 cm) cucumber
2 avocados
3½ ounces (100 g) baby spinach
10-13 fluid ounces (300-400 ml)
   water
2 tablespoons parsley, chopped
½ bunch fresh basil
2 tablespoons chives, chopped
½ tablespoon lime juice
a pinch of salt

Cut up cucumber and avocado in large chunks.

In a blender or food processor mix spinach and water, starting with 10 fluid ounces (300 ml) of water. Add remaining ingredients and blend again. Add more water little by little to get the right consistency, and taste to see if it needs more lime or salt.

Three-Day Menu—Perfect for a Weekend

Research shows it takes three days before white sugar leaves the body's systems, so therefore it can be beneficial to detox for a few days to clear out a little extra. This will give you a fresh start in less than a week, but still with a little more cleansing than the one-day program provides.

You may want to start the three-day program on a Friday. It can be quite exciting and interesting to do a thing like this over a weekend, so please choose a time when you have nothing else booked. You might even start your new week with a new perspective and a lot of energy!

As I already mentioned, even though the food is already blended to make it easier on the digestive system, it is important to remember to chew anyway!

The fat in the three-day program comes from nuts, avocados, and oils. If you want to do a more thorough cleanse, you can either opt out of the nuts or do the one-day program for three consecutive days, and then only eat fruits and vegetables.

Please feel free to try the three-day program if you are curious or to get a little taste of how the three weeks can look and feel.

DAY 1

BREAKFAST **Apple cereal**
1 serving (see page 72)

SNACK **Blue-green smoothie**
1 serving (see page 72)

LUNCH **Greek cauliflower**

Serves 2

Raw cauliflower grinds nicely in a food processor and is delicious mixed with fresh herbs and spices.

½ head cauliflower
2 tomatoes
4 inches (10 cm) cucumber
½ red bell pepper
½ bunch of mint
½ bunch of cilantro
½ bunch of basil
¼ cup (50 ml) chives
10 black olives, pitted
½ box of sunflower shoots,
   about 1.5 ounce (45 grams)
1 tablespoon olive oil
½ tablespoon lime juice

Cut the cauliflower into large pieces and pulse in the food processor until it becomes couscous-like. Cut tomatoes, cucumber, and bell pepper into pieces. Chop the herbs. Put everything in a bowl and add the olives and sunflower sprouts. Drizzle with oil and a squeeze of lime and mix again.

DINNER **Sushi with Brazil nuts and sauerkraut**

2 servings

Sauerkraut adds a lot of beneficial bacteria to the gut! One tablespoon a day is great for your stomach.

6 nori sheets
⅜ cup (75 ml) Brazil nuts
1 avocado
1 scant cup (200 ml) sauerkraut

Cut the nori sheets into 2 inch (5 cm) wide strips. Chop the nuts coarsely and dice the avocado. Mix with the sauerkraut. Place the mixture in nori strips and fold.

DAY 2

BREAKFAST **Apple cereal**
1 serving (see page 72)

LUNCH **Creamy zucchini pasta**
Serves 2
This dish resembles fettucini Alfredo with its creamy and tasty sauce for the zucchini.

2 zucchinis
1 ounce (25 g) of sprouted peas

Creamy Sauce:
½ cup (100 ml) pine nuts
2 tablespoons olive oil

1 tablespoon lemon juice
3-4 tablespoons water
a pinch of salt

Peel the zucchini with a potato peeler. Remove the outer green peel. Continue to peel to the core so that you get strips similar to tagliatelle. Place in a bowl and put a little salt on it. Blend the pine nuts until finely ground. Add olive oil, lemon, water, and a pinch of salt. Blend until you have a sauce. Pour the sauce over the zucchini. Add pea shoots on top.

SNACK **Energy soup**

1 serving
An energy soup is like a smoothie with sprouts as a base, and is both cleansing and strengthening.

1 celery stalk
1 apple
½ cucumber
1½ ounce (40 g) spinach
½ cup (100 ml) alfalfa
    sprouts
½ tablespoons lemon juice
1½ -2 cups (300-500 ml) water

½ avocado
herbal salt to taste

Cut celery, apple, and cucumber into pieces. Blend all ingredients except the avocado, starting with 1½ cup (300 ml) water. Add the avocado and blend again. Add more water if needed and flavor with herbal salt.

DINNER **Creamy carrot soup**

Serves 2
Seaweed is rich in minerals and helps to extract heavy metals from your body.

2.2 pounds (1 kg) carrots, or
    about 2 – 2½ cups store
    bought carrot juice
¾ inch (2 cm) fresh ginger
2 avocados
½ teaspoon cayenne pepper

Topping:
3 tablespoons flat-leaf parsley
½ cup (100 ml) arame seaweed

Soak the arame for 10 to 30 minutes. Pour off the water and rinse the seaweed. Juice the carrots in a juice extractor or use ready-squeezed juice. Peel the ginger and blend it with the carrot juice, avocado, and cayenne pepper. Finely chop the parsley and sprinkle it along with the seaweed as a topping for the soup.

DAY 3

BREAKFAST Apple cereal
1 serving (see page 72)

LUNCH AND DINNER Spinach soup
Serves 2 (see page 73)

SNACK Tangy carrot cake
Serves 4
A fresh and easy-to-make carrot cake!

¼ cup (50 ml) coconut oil
6 carrots
2 red apples
1 teaspoon ground vanilla bean
4 fresh dates
1 tablespoon lemon juice
zest of one lemon, finely grated

Garnish:
¼ cup (50 ml) goji berries

Make the coconut oil into liquid form (see page 69). Cut the carrots into large pieces and mix them in the food processor until they are coarsely chopped. Add the apple, cut into large pieces, and mix again. Add the remaining ingredients and process until all is mixed together. If needed, add more lemon and ground vanilla bean. Spread the batter on a platter and place in the fridge a few hours before serving. Garnish with goji berries.

Menu Week 1—Start Here

The three-week program includes an initial week, a cleansing week, and then an introductory week on raw food as a lifestyle. The recipes are based on all the wonderful ingredients that are available in raw food, so the menu can be as tasty and varied as possible. The dishes are simple to prepare, and the body gets all the nutrients, carbohydrates, fats, and proteins that it needs. Lunch is salad for all three weeks. On page 132, you can read more about how to create your own raw salad.

   If you want to implement a one-week program, I recommend that you choose the first week, since it's designed as a starting point. In seven days you have enough time to get a good feel for what it would feel like to eat raw and to detox for three weeks. But the one-week program can also act like a refreshing cleanse now and then, if you would like to reconnect with the pure food.

MONDAY

Preparation:
Soak the apricots 4 to 8 hours (for snack). You can soak the apricots on Saturday night to make the snack bars on Sunday and have them ready for Monday.

BREAKFAST **Kiwi breakfast**

1 serving
Celery gives us strong bones and restores the fluid balance in the body after a night of rest.

1 pear
2 celery stalks
2 yellow kiwi fruits
1 tablespoon water
½ teaspoon ground ginger

Cut pears, celery, and one of the kiwis into large pieces and mix in the blender with 1 tablespoon water until it is a smooth consistency. Top with the other kiwi, cut into pieces, and ground ginger.

SNACK **Almond bars**

4 bars

Consider making a double batch and freezing these. They are nice to have when you need a quick snack. Will keep for a week in the fridge and for three months in the freezer.

1½ cup almonds
½ cup shredded coconut
1 teaspoon cinnamon
1 pinch cardamom
1 pinch ginger
3 dates
5 apricots, soaked

Pulse the almonds to a fine flour in a small food processor. Add the coconut and spices and continue blending. Add dates and apricots and continue until all is blended. Shape into rectangular bars—this will be easier with the help of parchment paper!

DINNER **Zucchini with pumpkin pesto**

2-3 servings

Once the pesto is made, this is a dinner that you can put together in less than five minutes. The zucchini pasta can be made quickly using a potato peeler. Expect to use one zucchini per person.

1-2 zucchinis

Pumpkin pesto:
½ cup (100 ml) pumpkin seeds
⅜ cup (75 ml) olive oil
1 tablespoon lemon juice
1 pinch salt
1 bunch of basil

Topping:
7 black olives
5 cherry tomatoes

In a food processor, pulse the pumpkin seeds into a fine flour. Add olive oil, lemon, and salt, and mix until well blended. Stop occasionally to scrape down the sides. Add the basil leaves. Season with more olive oil, salt, and lemon. Store the pesto in a sealed jar. It will last for about a week in the refrigerator.

   Peel the outside of the green zucchini with a potato peeler. Continue peeling to the core. Save the core and use it for your next day lunch salad. Stir zucchini and pesto together and top with olives and cherry tomatoes.

TUESDAY

Preparation:
Soak five sun-dried tomatoes for 2 to 4 hours (for dinner).

BREAKFAST **Kiwi breakfast**
1 serving (see page 80)

SNACK **Apple sandwich with goji berries**
2 servings
Sandwiches are a common snack. A raw food sandwich alternative is to slice an apple, spread it with a good tahini, and then top with the super food goji berries!

2 apples

Tahini:
½ cup (100 ml) sesame seeds
1-2 tablespoons your choice of oil
1 tablespoon desiccated coconut
1 tablespoon coconut oil

Topping:
2 tablespoons goji berries

Soften the coconut oil (it doesn't have to be liquid). Mix the sesame seeds in the blender until they are finely ground, add 1 to 2 tablespoons oil, and blend again until you have a smooth paste. Mix the sesame paste with coconut flakes and coconut oil. Cut the apples into slices and spread them with tahini. Top with goji berries.

DINNER **Chili and walnut rolls**

2-3 servings
A spicy nut dip with fresh chili!

5 sheets of nori

Dip:
1½ cups (350 ml) walnuts
2 carrots
5 sun-dried tomatoes, soaked
¼-½ fresh chili
½ cup (100 ml) oregano, fresh
¼ red pepper
1 tablespoon lemon juice

½ cup (100 ml) sauerkraut

Cut the nori sheets into 2-inch (5 cm) wide strips. Pulse the walnuts in food processor until they are coarsely chopped. Add coarsely chopped carrots. Add the sun-dried tomatoes, chilies, oregano, pepper, and lemon and mix until smooth. Put the dip in a bowl.

How to make rolls: Take a strip of nori and add about 3 tablespoons nut dip and ½ tablespoon sauerkraut. Roll up and repeat to make about 10 rolls. Make more if you're extra hungry. You can vary this recipe by putting the dip on leaves of romaine lettuce.

Use a large food processor if you make the recipe as is, and if you only do half for one dinner serving then use a small food processor.

WEDNESDAY

Preparation:

Soak the raisins, 4 hours (for snack).

Soak the almonds, 8 hours (for snack).

Soak 2 cups buckwheat for 8 hours (enough for both Wednesday's and Thursday's snack). Rinse the buckwheat thoroughly after 8 hours. Let half of it sprout in the fridge until Thursday (for snack).

BREAKFAST Apple cereal

1 portion (see page 72)

SNACK Buckwheat with raisins and almonds

1 serving

This is one of my favorite snacks that I vary with whatever kind of fruit, berries, or nuts I have on hand! This will keep you going until dinner.

¼ cup (50 ml) almonds, soaked

1 red apple

½ cup (100 ml) buckwheat, soaked

2 tablespoons raisins, soaked

½ teaspoon cinnamon

Chop the almonds coarsely and cut the apple into small pieces. Mix all ingredients in a bowl and eat!

DINNER **Parsnip couscous with pumpkin seeds**

1 serving

Because I can buy organic and locally grown parsnips year-round, it is one of the roots that I use the most.

1 small parsnip
½ tablespoon olive oil
a dash of lemon juice, a pinch of salt
1.5 ounce (35 g) arugula
1 pear
2 tablespoons pumpkin seeds

Peel the parsnip and cut it into large pieces. Mix it in the food processor until it becomes the consistency of couscous. Add the olive oil, lemon, and salt and mix again for a short time. Put everything in a bowl. Rinse the arugula and mix into the parsnip couscous. Add the pear, cut into pieces, along with pumpkin seeds.

THURSDAY

Preparation:

Buckwheat should be soaked and sprouted (for snack).

Soak apricots, 8 hours (for snack).

Soak sunflower seeds, 8 hours (for snack).

Thaw blueberries if you do not use fresh (for snack).

BREAKFAST **Apple cereal**

1 portion (see page 72)

SNACK **Fruity buckwheat**

1 serving
This is almost like a raw version of rice pudding with blueberries!

½ cup (100 ml) blueberries (fresh or frozen that have been thawed)
3 apricots, soaked
½ cup (100 ml) buckwheat, soaked and sprouted
2 tablespoons sunflower seeds, soaked

Blend blueberries and apricots in the blender. Add buckwheat and sunflower seeds and blend again.

DINNER **Spinach soup**

Serves 2
The spinach soup is smooth and satisfying, and your whole body will thank you for it. The recipe is enough for two people or one very hungry person!

4 inches (10 cm) cucumber
2 avocados
3.5 ounces (100 g) baby spinach
1¼-1¾ cups (300-400 ml) water
2 tablespoons parsley, chopped
½ bunch of fresh basil
2 tablespoons chives, chopped
½ tablespoon lime juice
a pinch of salt

Cut cucumber and avocado in large chunks. Mix spinach, and then water, starting with 1¼ cups water. Add remaining ingredients and blend again. Add more water as needed to get the right texture. Taste to see if it needs more lime or salt.

FRIDAY

Preparation:

Soak cranberries, 4-8 hours (for snack).

Thaw raspberries if you do not use fresh (for snack).

Soak the sun-dried tomatoes, 4 hours (for dinner).

BREAKFAST **Apple cereal**

1 portion (see page 72)

SNACK **Cranberry cream**

1 serving

Cranberries are rich in antioxidants. They are similar to raisins, but have a tarter flavor.

1 avocado

½ cup (100 ml) cranberries, soaked

1-2 teaspoons lemon juice

½ cup (100 ml) raspberries, fresh or frozen

Mix together avocado, cranberry, and lemon juice. Add water if needed to get a creamy consistency. Place in a bowl and top with raspberries.

DINNER **Cashew dip with vegetables**

2-3 servings

Friday night yummies with vegetable sticks and dip!

Dip:

2 cups (500 ml) cashews

4 inches (10 cm) leek

1½ ounce (40 g) arugula

8 sun-dried tomatoes, soaked

Vegetables:

cucumber

celery

carrot

Pulse the cashew nuts into a fine flour in a food processor. Rinse leeks thoroughly and cut into pieces. Put them in a food processor with the cashews, add arugula and sun-dried tomatoes, and process until well blended. Stop occasionally to scrape down the sides. Add a little water if it gets too dry. Cut the carrots, cucumber, and celery into sticks and eat with the dip.

SATURDAY

Preparation:
Soak the hazelnuts, 8 hours (for snack).
Thaw blackberries and raspberries, if using frozen (for breakfast and snack).
Soak the sun-dried tomatoes (if they are not in oil), 4 hours (for dinner).

BREAKFAST Blackberries and fennel

1 serving of blackberries, dark purple and shiny, will brighten your morning.

1 apple
½ fennel
¼ cup (50 ml) water
½ cup (100 ml) blackberries

Cut the apple and fennel into pieces and mix with water in a blender. Serve topped with blackberries.

SNACK Saturday pie

2 servings
Carob and raspberry pie makes a special Saturday treat!

¼ cup (50 ml) shredded coconut
½ cup (100 ml) hazelnuts, soaked
  6 dates
a pinch of salt
1½ tablespoons carob powder
½ teaspoon ground vanilla bean

Filling:
1 scant cup (200 ml) raspberries

In a food processor, pulse coconut and nuts to a fine powder. Add the dates, salt, carob, and ground vanilla bean, and process again until it becomes like a dough. Press out on a small plate or in individual pie plates and fill with raspberries. You can make pie crusts for two servings, and then freeze one. I'm sure you have a friend that you could treat to a delicious pie sometime!

DINNER **Cabbage wraps**

1 serving
These wraps are good, quick to make, and a perfect lunch to bring to work.

a head of cabbage
3 carrots

Sun-dried tomatoes mixture:
1 scant cup (200 ml) sun-dried tomatoes, soaked
¼ cup (50 ml) olive oil (exclude if you use tomatoes in oil)

Avocado dressing:
1 avocado
2 dates
½ tablespoon apple cider vinegar
¾ cup (150 ml) water
2 teaspoons lime juice

Separate cabbage leaves—how many you use depends on how hungry you are
and how large your cabbage is.

Grate the carrots coarsely and put them in a bowl. Mix the sun-dried
tomatoes with the oil into a consistency resembling pesto or tapenade.

Blend the ingredients for the avocado dressing to a smooth consistency.
Place in a bowl. Take a cabbage leaf and put on some shredded carrots and a
dab of sun-dried tomato paste. Top with avocado sauce and roll it all together
into a wrap.

SUNDAY

Preparation:

Thaw blackberries, if using frozen (for breakfast).

Thaw strawberries, if using frozen (for snack).

Soak figs, 4 hours (for snack).

Soak sun-dried tomatoes, 4 hours (for dinner).

BREAKFAST **Blackberries and fennel**

1 serving (see recipe page 93)

SNACK **Sesame milk with strawberries**

Serves 2

Experiment to find out how thick you want the sesame milk. I like it really creamy—then it becomes sesame cream with strawberries!

½ cup (100 ml) sesame seeds

1½ cups (300 ml) water

2 figs, soaked

1 scant cup (200 ml) strawberries, frozen or fresh

In a food processor, process sesame seeds into a fine flour. Add water and mix into a milk-like consistency. Add the figs and mix again. Serve with strawberries.

DINNER **Lasagna with crispy cabbage salad**

Serves 4

Sunday dinner consists of wholesome lasagna and a crunchy coleslaw.

2 large zucchini

Seed mixture:
1¾ cup (400 ml) pumpkin
seeds
1½ cup (300 ml) sunflower
seeds
½-1 tablespoon paprika
2 teaspoons cumin
1 teaspoon chili powder
1 tablespoon canola oil
½ tablespoon lemon juice
a pinch of salt

Tomato sauce:
4 tomatoes
12 sun-dried tomatoes, soaked

Topping:
1 large avocado or 2 small

Cabbage salad:
½ head of cabbage
1 tablespoon apple cider vinegar
1 tablespoon olive oil
a pinch of salt
two or three turns of pepper mill

Make "lasagna" of zucchini by slicing it with a cheese slicer. Mix the pumpkin seeds and sunflower seeds in food processor until they are coarsely chopped. Add spices, rapeseed (or olive) oil, lemon juice, and salt and mix again until well blended. Season to taste.

Mix tomatoes and sun-dried tomatoes into a sauce in the blender.

Cover the bottom of a clear casserole dish with the zucchini. Spread the tomato sauce and seed mixture on top. Repeat and finish with a layer of zucchini. Cut the avocado into slices and put on top.

Shred the cabbage finely and toss it with apple cider vinegar, oil, and salt. Season with black pepper. Serve with the lasagna.

Menu Week 2 - More Cleansing!

This week we will focus more on cleansing, which means green smoothies, soups, and not a whole lot of nuts and seeds. Green smoothies consist of mixed leafy greens and fruit. In the back of the book you will find a list of books to read, including *Green for Life,* which is great if you want to know more about green smoothies. Drink herbal tea or chew on licorice root if you get a craving for something. The lettuce is still in our lunches because we still need to chew, but omit the avocado in the salad this week. For a variation, you may serve your salad with a dressing made with nuts or seeds. If you have the motivation and want to focus on weight loss, eat the salad as it is with a tablespoon of oil and lemon juice, and seaweed and sauerkraut.

MONDAY

Preparation:
Soak the figs, 4 hours (for snack).

BREAKFAST Zucchini breakfast

1 serving

Zucchini gives us different minerals that make our body feel really good. It's great to start the day with a creamy fruit cereal that gives the body what it needs to function at its best!

½ zucchini
1 pear
1 apple
optional: cinnamon and ground ginger

Cut zucchini and pears into large chunks and blend in the food processor. Add the apple, cut into large chunks, and continue blending to a smooth consistency. Serve in a bowl and sprinkle with cinnamon and ginger.

SNACK A substantial snack

2 servings

Figs and walnuts are excellent together and even better served on sliced pear.

Fig mix:
¼ cup (50 ml) walnuts
5 figs, soaked
½ teaspoon cinnamon
½-¾ inch (1-2 cm) of fresh
   ginger, grated
2 teaspoons lemon juice
1 pinch nutmeg
¼-½ cup (50-100 ml)
   soaking water from figs

Serve with:
1 pear

Pulse the walnuts in a food processor. Add the figs and continue blending. Add the remaining ingredients and mix until well blended. Cut the pear into slices and spread the mixture on them.

DINNER **Greek Cauliflower**

Serves 2

Raw cauliflower is delicious minced in the food processor and paired with fresh herbs and spices.

1 head cauliflower
2 tomatoes
4 inches (10 cm) cucumber
½ red bell pepper
½ bunch of mint
½ bunch of cilantro
½ bunch of basil
¼ cup (50 ml) chives
10 black olives
½ container of sunflower shoots, about 1.5 ounce (45 g)
1 tablespoon olive oil
½ tablespoon lime juice

Cut the cauliflower into large pieces and pulse in the food processor until the consistency resembles couscous. Cut tomatoes, cucumber, and bell pepper into pieces. Chop the herbs. Combine everything in a bowl and add the olives and sunflower sprouts. Drizzle with oil and a squeeze of lime, and toss together.

TUESDAY

Preparation:
Thaw the blackberries, or use frozen for a cool drink (for snacks).
Soak apricots, 4 hours (for snack).

BREAKFAST Zucchini breakfast
1 serving (see page 99)

SNACK Blackberries with Brazil nut yogurt
1 serving
Fancy a milkshake? Make the nut milk slightly thicker and use half the amount of thawed berries.

Nut milk:
½ cup (100 ml) Brazil nuts
1½ cups (300 ml) water
¼ cup (50 ml) blackberries, frozen or semi-thawed
1 tablespoon açai powder (optional)
2 apricots, soaked
1 pinch salt

Mix Brazil nuts in water to a milk-like consistency and strain through wire strainer or nut milk bag. Blend with all other ingredients until you have a smoothie.

DINNER **Sushi light**

2 servings

I really like to eat with my hands. When you eat raw sushi there's no need for knife, fork, or chopsticks!

1 parsnip
2 carrots
1 yellow bell pepper
¼ large or 1 small papaya
2 avocados, cut in small pieces
6 sheets of nori

Serve with:
wasabi paste and tamari to taste

Peel the parsnip. Slice the parsnips, carrots, and peppers and then cut the papaya into 2 inch (5 cm) long pieces. Cut the avocado into thin slices as well. Place the vegetables on a platter.

Cut the nori sheets into 2 inch (5 cm) wide strips.

Serve tamari and wasabi in separate bowls. Put a stick of each vegetable on the nori with some wasabi and roll up. Dip the roll in the tamari immediately before you eat.

WEDNESDAY

Preparation:

Thaw blueberries, if using frozen (for breakfast).

Soak figs, 4 hours (for snack).

Soak the seaweed, 10 to 30 minutes (for dinner).

BREAKFAST **Blue-green breakfast**

1 serving

Chlorophyll is what makes spinach green—it's like sunshine concentrate.

Can you start your day more radiantly?

½ pear
½ cup (100 ml) blueberries
2.5 ounces (70 g) baby spinach
1½-2 cups (300-500 ml) water
½ avocado

Cut the pear into large pieces and mix with blueberries, spinach, and water until well blended. Start with 1½ cups (300 ml) water. Add avocado and blend again. Add more water if needed.

SNACK **Green smoothie with figs**

1 serving

Pour your green smoothies in nice glass bottles, recycled glass jars, or thermoses to make you even happier when you drink them.

2.5 ounces (70 g) baby spinach
1½-2 cups (300-500 ml) water
1 pear
2 figs, soaked

Blend spinach with 1½ cups (300 ml) water. Cut the pear, add along with the figs, and blend again. Add more water if needed to find the right consistency for your smoothie.

DINNER **Creamy carrot soup**

Serves 2 (see recipe page 77)

THURSDAY

Preparation:

Thaw blueberries, if using frozen (for breakfast).

BREAKFAST **Blue-green breakfast**

1 serving (see recipe page 105)

SNACK **Energy soup**

1 portion

This snack has a green, fresh taste from the sour apple and a smooth creaminess from the avocado. Works equally well for snack, breakfast, and lunch!

1 celery stalk
1 apple
½ cucumber
1½ ounces (40 g) of spinach
½ cup (100 ml) alfalfa sprouts
2 tablespoons lemon juice
1½-2 cups (300-500 ml) water
½ avocado
herbal salt

Cut up celery, apple, and cucumber into medium-sized pieces. Mix together all ingredients except for the avocado. Add the avocado and blend. Add more water if needed and some herbal salt.

DINNER **Gazpacho**

Serves 2

Traditionally gazpacho is served cold, often or with an ice cube. A cool and refreshing raw dinner on a hot summer day!

1 yellow onion
1 large red bell pepper
1 large green bell pepper
1 small cucumber or ½ large
3 large tomatoes
3 tablespoons lemon juice
½ bunch of fresh basil
1 tablespoon olive oil
herbal salt to taste

Peel and cut the onion in half. Let it sit in a bowl of cold water for 30 minutes. Rinse the onion. Cut the peppers into large pieces and add together with the onion to the food processor. Pulse until roughly chopped. Cut the cucumber in large chunks and add. Pulse again. Cut the tomatoes, add them, and pulse for another several seconds. Add the lemon juice, basil, and olive oil and process until well blended. The soup will still have a slightly rough texture. Season with herbal salt. You can make the gazpacho the day before—it actually tastes better if it's left to sit for a while. You can also freeze it, so you will have servings ready whenever you need.

FRIDAY

Preparation:

Thaw blueberries, if using frozen (for breakfast).
Soak sunflower seeds for 4 to 8 hours (for dinner).

BREAKFAST **Blue-green breakfast**

1 serving (see recipe page 105)

SNACK **Beautiful green smoothie**

2 servings

Three kinds of greens: parsley, romaine lettuce, and avocado! If you choose green apples, it makes a completely green smoothie. Green is good!

2 apples
1 head romaine lettuce
2 cups (500 ml) of water
a bunch of parsley
1 avocado
2 tablespoons lemon juice

Cut the apple into large chunks and cut the lettuce roughly. Blend all ingredients except for the avocado and lemon juice. Add the avocado and lemon juice and blend again until you have a creamy smoothie.

DINNER **Zucchini rolls with dill paste**

2 servings

Dill can vary greatly in flavor. Sometimes I buy dill that barely tastes like anything at all, and sometimes it tastes very strong. So "dill" it up to your liking!

Dill paste:
2 cups (500 ml) sunflower seeds, soaked
1-2 tablespoons lemon juice
a bunch of dill

Vegetables:
1 zucchini
2 carrots
1¾ ounce (50 g) of alfalfa sprouts

Serve with:
wasabi paste to taste
¼ cup (50 ml) tamari

Mix sunflower seeds in a food processor until they are coarsely chopped. Add the lemon juice and dill and process until it becomes a creamy paste. You may have to add a little water.

Slice the zucchini with a cheese slicer sideways (remove the first slice with the peel on), and cut the carrots into thin strips. Spread the mixture on the zucchini slices, and add carrots and sprouts and a little wasabi. Roll them up. Dip the rolls in tamari when you are ready to eat them.

SATURDAY

Preparation:

Thaw raspberries and blackberries, if using frozen (for breakfast).

BREAKFAST Blue and yellow breakfast

1 serving

This is how you know if a mango is ripe enough: hold it in your hand and squeeze gently. If there's a soft resistance, it's ripe; if it feels too soft, it's overripe; and if it's hard, it's not ripe yet.

1 mango
¼ cup (50 ml) raspberries
¼ cup (50 ml) blackberries

Cut the mango into small pieces. Toss with the berries and place on a beautiful plate.

SNACK **Tangy carrot cake**

Serves 4
A fresh and easy carrot cake!

6 carrots
2 red apples
1 teaspoon ground vanilla bean
¼ cup (50 ml) coconut oil
4 fresh dates
1 tablespoon lemon juice
zest of one lemon, finely grated

Garnish:
¼ cup (50 ml) goji berries

Make the coconut oil liquid (see page 69). Cut the carrots into large pieces and pulse them in a food processor until coarse. Add apple, cut in large pieces, and pulse again. Add the remaining ingredients and process until well blended. Season to taste with more lemon juice and ground vanilla bean. Spread on a platter and place in the fridge a few hours before serving. Garnish with goji berries.

DINNER **Stuffed peppers with curry avocado**

2 servings
Peppers that don't need to go in the oven!

2 red peppers
1 avocado
2 stalks celery
½ cucumber
1 tomato
2 spring onions
1 teaspoon curry powder
½ teaspoon each of cumin,
    coriander, chervil, and
    herbal salt
½ teaspoon tamari
1 teaspoon lemon juice

1.25 ounces (35 g) arugula
2 tablespoons parsley

Cut the peppers in half and take the seeds out. Dice the avocado, celery, cucumber, and tomato, and chop the onion. Mix the vegetables and onions with spices, tamari, and lemon. Fill pepper halves with the mixture. Make a bed of arugula on individual plates and put the peppers on top. Garnish with chopped parsley.

SUNDAY

Preparation:

Thaw raspberries, if using frozen (for snack).
Soak goji berries, about 30 minutes (for dinner).

BREAKFAST Blue-green breakfast

1 serving (see recipe page 105)

SNACK Carob mousse with avocado

1 serving

Carob, which is similar to chocolate in flavor, replaces cocoa in this recipe. The smooth and soft coconut oil adds extra creaminess and flavor.
Mmmmm . . . To prepare a single serving, use a small food processor.

1 tablespoon coconut oil
½ cup (100 ml) water
5 dates
1 tablespoon carob powder
½ teaspoon ground vanilla bean
1 avocado

Serve with:
¼ cup (50 ml) raspberries,
    fresh or frozen and thawed

Make the coconut oil liquid over a warm double boiler. Mix water and dates in the food processor. Add the coconut oil, carob powder, and ground vanilla bean and mix again. Finally, add the avocado and mix for a short while. Serve in a bowl with the raspberries.

DINNER **Parsley tabouleh with pistachios and goji berries**

Serves 4

When I eat parsley tabouleh, which I do a lot, I smile—I smile to myself in the mirror to see if any little green goodies are stuck between my teeth.

¼ cup (50 ml) goji berries, soaked
one bunch curly parsley
a bunch or two bunches flat leaf parsley
2 avocados
½ cup (100 ml) pistachios
2 tablespoons olive oil
2 tablespoons lemon juice
a pinch of salt

Prepare by soaking the goji berries for 30 minutes. Chop all the parsley, cut the avocado into small pieces, and roughly chop the pistachios. Gently mix together with the goji berries. Drizzle with oil, lemon juice, and salt. Toss well again and serve!

Menu Week 3—
Final Week of Your Fresh Start.

After a week that focused on cleansing, you have arrived at the last week of the program. You are now starting to eat some more nuts and seeds again, but it is still salad for lunch.

By now you've probably got the hang of how the various elements of the preparation of the food is done. Also, try to sense and feel how your taste buds have changed, as they renew every seven days. Feel the flavors and allow your body to fully enjoy the lifestyle change that you are in the midst of.

Ask yourself some questions during this week: What do you like? What would you like to take with you to your regular diet? Was breakfast best, or maybe that little bit of time you took to make a yummy and healthy snack each day?

MONDAY
Preparation:

Soak the prunes, 4 hours (for breakfast).

Soak the raisins, 4 hours (for snack).

Soak 1½ cups (300 ml) green lentils for 8 hours, discard water, and rinse.

Let sprout until Wednesday. Rinse once a day.

BREAKFAST **Breakfast with fennel and prunes**

Serves 2

The superberry, açai, gives this breakfast some extra oomph and charges it with antioxidants. Make variations with rosehip or nettle powder.

½ fennel bulb
2 small apples or one large
1 pear
6 prunes, soaked
1 tablespoon açai powder/rose hip powder/nettle powder

Cut the fennel, apple, and pear coarsely and mix all ingredients in the food processor with some of the soaking water to the desired mushy texture.

SNACK **Spice balls**

10-15 balls

Just like small Christmas delights, you'll want to eat these snack balls all day!

1 scant cup (200 ml) almonds
1½ cups (300 ml) sunflower seeds
½ cup (100 ml) pumpkin seeds
2 teaspoons ground ginger
2 teaspoons ground cloves
2 tablespoons cinnamon
a pinch of salt
¼ cup (50 ml) coconut oil
1¾ cup (400 ml) raisins, soaked

Pulse almonds, sunflower seeds, and pumpkin seeds in food processor until they are finely minced. Add spices and salt and process again. Make coconut oil into liquid over a warm double boiler. Add the coconut and raisins, and process until well blended. Squeeze into balls and refrigerate. The coconut oil will make the balls solidify.

DINNER **Yellow cauliflower**

2 servings

Mashed cauliflower with curry is so beautiful in color. Served with bright, crunchy pea shoots and avocado, you get a nicely green and cheerfully yellow meal!

1 head cauliflower
2 teaspoons lime juice
a pinch of salt
1 tablespoon olive oil
1-2 tablespoons curry
1 yellow bell pepper
1¾ ounce (50 g) of pea shoots
¼ cup (50 ml) sunflower seeds
1 avocado

Cut the cauliflower into small florets. Pulse in the food processor until finely chopped. Add the lime juice, salt, olive oil, and curry and process again until everything is well blended. Put in a bowl. Cut the peppers into chunks and mix into the cauliflower mixture with the pea shoots and sunflower kernels. Serve with avocado.

TUESDAY

Preparation:

Soak the prunes, 8 hours (for breakfast).
Soak walnuts, 8 hours (for snack).
Soak the sun-dried tomatoes, 4 hours (for dinner).

BREAKFAST **Breakfast with fennel and prunes**

Serves 2 (see recipe page 115)

SNACK **Celery snack**

1 serving

We want more celery! With apples and walnuts this will remind you of a Waldorf salad.

1 apple
1 celery stalk
¼ cup (50 ml) walnuts, soaked

Cut the apple and celery into small pieces and roughly chop the walnuts. Mix all ingredients together.

DINNER **Zucchini and carrot pasta with almond tapenade**

Serves 4

With a jar of ready-made tapenade in the refrigerator, dinner is ready in no time. It's also great on flax seed crackers, topped with cucumber slices.

Almond tapenade:
2 cups almonds
7 sun-dried tomatoes, soaked
¼ cup (50 ml) olive oil
a pinch of salt

2 zucchinis
4 carrots

Process the almonds in the blender until they become flour, then add all other ingredients. If your blender is not very powerful, you may have to push the mixture down a bit, or otherwise use the food processor. The consistency should be like a tapenade. Put the paste in a bowl.

Peel the zucchini and carrots and continue to peel all the way to the cores so you get long vegetable slices. Serve with the almond tapenade.

WEDNESDAY

Preparation:

Rinse the sprouted lentils, if you sprout your own (for breakfast).

Soak the almonds, 8 hours (for snack).

Soak apricots, 4 to 8 hours (for snack).

Thaw berries, or use frozen if you want the smoothie cold (for snack).

BREAKFAST **Sprouted breakfast**

1 serving

Green sprouted lentils are my favorite sprouts, and they taste really good with apples. Eating this cereal in the morning makes you feel wonderfully satisfied for hours.

2 apples

½ cup (100 ml) sprouted green lentils

¼ cup (50 ml) water + possibly a little more

cinnamon to taste

Prepare by sprouting the green lentils 2 to 3 days in advance (see "Preparation," page 114) or buy ready-made sprouts in the store. Mix apples, cut into rough pieces with sprouts and as much water as needed to reach desired consistency. Place in a bowl and sprinkle the cinnamon on top.

SNACK **Lingonberry smoothie**

1 portion
When it's hot outside and you want something cool, use frozen lingonberries.

1-1½ cups (200-300 ml) water
½ cup (100 ml) almonds, soaked
2 apricots, soaked
¼ cup (50 ml) lingonberries, frozen or thawed

Translator's note: Lingonberries are very similar to cranberries in flavor and texture.

Blend together 1 scant cup (200 ml) water with almonds to make a milk. Strain through a mesh sieve or a nut milk bag. Pour the strained milk into the blender. Add apricots and blend again. Blend in the berries and add more water to desired consistency.

DINNER **Broccoli and apple pie with curry**
Serves 2

Typically, pies contain eggs, gluten, and dairy products. Without these ingredients, they taste better and your body will also be happier.

Filling:
½ bunch of broccoli
1 green apple
1 avocado
lemon juice and salt to taste
optional: tamari

Cut broccoli and apple into pieces and pulse in the food processor until they are coarsely chopped. Add the avocado and process until you have a creamy texture. Season with lemon and salt. Place the filling in a pie pan. If you want an even saltier flavor, you may serve it with tamari.

Pie topping:
¼ cup (50 ml) pumpkin seeds
½ cup (100 ml) sunflower seeds
a pinch of salt
½ teaspoon curry powder
1 tablespoon olive oil

Process the seeds in food processor until they are finely chopped. Add salt, curry powder, and olive oil and season. Put the pie topping on top of the filling.

THURSDAY

Preparation:

Rinse the sprouts, if you make your own (for breakfast).

Soak the raisins, 4 to 8 hours (for snack).

Thaw the lingonberries, if using frozen (for dinner).

Soak the pumpkin seeds, 4 to 8 hours (for dinner).

BREAKFAST **Sprouted breakfast**

1 serving (see recipe page 118)

SNACK **Spirulina balls**

10-15 balls

Spirulina is a type of seaweed sold in the form of a powder. The balls are green and yummy with a tangy taste of lemon. Hazelnuts, raisins, spirulina, and lemon have an alkaline effect on the body.

3 cups (700 ml) hazelnuts

1½ cups (300 ml) raisins, soaked

2 tablespoons coconut oil, grated

lemon zest from 2 lemons

1 tablespoon spirulina powder (if you are brave, add some more . . .)

Pulse the hazelnuts in a food processor until they are ground. Add the raisins and process again. Add the coconut oil, lemon zest, and spirulina powder. Roll into bite-sized balls, or eat as is.

DINNER **Cabbage with cranberry**

1 serving

My favorite dinner is cabbage—as a main course or as a side dish. Cabbage is a nutritious food because it contains a lot of glucosinolates, which help to effectively clean your liver. Furthermore, cabbage is rich in vitamin C and other antioxidants, not to mention fiber.

½ small head of cabbage
1 tablespoon olive oil
2 teaspoons lemon juice
½ tablespoon apple cider vinegar
½ cup (100 ml) cranberries, fresh or frozen and thawed
¼ cup (50 ml) pumpkin seeds, soaked

Shred the cabbage finely and place in a bowl. Pour in olive oil, lemon juice and apple cider vinegar. Mix with your hands until the cabbage softens. Add the cranberries and pumpkin seeds and mix.

FRIDAY

Preparation:

Rinse sprouts, if you make your own (for breakfast).
Soak sun-dried tomatoes, 4 hours (for dinner).
Soak dried apricots, 4 to 8 hours (for dinner).

BREAKFAST **Sprouted breakfast**

1 serving (see recipe page 118)

SNACK **P & P snack**

1 serving

Papaya and pecans face each other in a phenomenal combination. A pear is icing on the cake, or maybe just an extra p!?

¼ large papaya or ½ small
1 pear
¼ cup (50 ml) pecans

Cut papaya and pears into pieces, and chop the nuts coarsely. Place all ingredients in a pretty bowl.

DINNER **Tomato soup**

Serves 2

Garlic and chili gives an extra kick to this! But if you're a softy like me and like mild flavor, opt out of those hot ones.

3 tomatoes
1 avocado
1½ carrot
1 stalk celery
optional: ¼ red onion
¼ cup (50 ml) sun-dried tomatoes, soaked
½-1 scant cup (100-200 ml) water
3 dried apricots, soaked
2 tablespoons olive oil
2 teaspoons tamari/name shoyu
2 tablespoons fresh basil
¼-½ red chili without seeds
1 clove garlic

Cut the tomatoes, avocado, carrot, celery, and if you chose to, red onion in large pieces. Mix the tomatoes. Add the remaining ingredients gradually, adding the avocado last. Be careful with the chili and garlic. Season to taste.

SATURDAY

Preparation:
Thaw blueberries, if you do not use fresh (for breakfast).
Soak the Brazil nuts, 8 to 12 hours (for dinner).

BREAKFAST Avocado and berries

A beautiful, pale pear and the dark, flavorful blueberries paired with a mild avocado make for a very yummy breakfast.

1 avocado
1 pear
3½ ounces (100 g) blueberries

Cut the avocados and pears into pieces. Mix together in a bowl and top with blueberries.

SNACK Mulberry apples

Mulberries contain a substance that regulates blood sugar levels, and the little berries taste like caramel.

2 apples
1 teaspoon cinnamon
½ teaspoon cardamom
4 tablespoons mulberries

Grate the apples coarsely and mix with the spices. Add the mulberries and let sit for half an hour before serving.

DINNER Sushi with Brazil nuts and sauerkraut

2 servings (see recipe page 75)

SUNDAY

Preparation:

Thaw blueberries, if using frozen (for breakfast).

Soak figs, 4 to 8 hours (for snack).

Soak apricots, 4 to 8 hours (for dinner).

Soak sun-dried tomatoes, 4 hours (for dinner).

BREAKFAST **Avocado with berries**
(see recipe page 127)

SNACK **Soft carob cake**
2-4 servings
A soft nougat-like cream on a dark and juicy bottom, topped with flakes of dried coconut—so good, so good! Enjoy a wonderful cake on the final day of a three-week lifestyle change.

Cake layer:
2 cups (500 ml) figs, soaked
2 cups (500 ml) walnuts
1¼ cup carob powder

Cream:
1½ cups (300 ml) cashews
1½ cups water
6 dates
¼ cup (50 ml) carob powder
½ avocado

Topping:
½ cup (100 ml) shredded coconut

Pulse the figs in a food processor until minced. Add the walnuts and process until it becomes a creamy paste. Add carob powder and mix again. Shape into a round, tall cake on a platter, or use a spring-form pan.

Grind cashew nuts to a fine flour in blender. Add water, dates, and carob powder and blend again. Add the avocado and mix one last time until you have a cream. You may have to scrape down the cream from the sides. Spread the cream on the bottom and top with grated coconut.

DINNER **Curry rice with apricots, yogurt with bell pepper, and hot apple chutney**

Serves 2

The parsnip gives you calcium that provides strong bones! Take a closer look at this root vegetable, and you will see that it actually resembles a bone.

2 parsnips
½ teaspoon curry powder
½ teaspoon cumin
½ tablespoon lemon juice
a pinch of salt
1 tablespoon olive oil
7 apricots, soaked (save the soaking
   water for the chutney)
¼ cup (50 ml) sunflower seeds

Peel and cut parsnips into pieces and then pulse in the food processor until they get a rice-like consistency. Add the curry, cumin, lemon juice, salt, and olive oil, and pulse again. Place into a bowl and add apricots and sunflower seeds. Serve with apple chutney and bell pepper yogurt.

Apple chutney with chili

1 large apple or 2 small
3 tablespoons apple cider vinegar
2 tablespoons soaking water from
   the apricots
½ inch red chili
2 tablespoons grated ginger

Cut the apples coarsely and mix them in food processor until they are coarsely chopped. Add the apple cider vinegar, soaking water, chili, and ginger until well blended. Make chutney as hot as you please. The consistency should be like a coarse applesauce.

Yogurt with bell peppers
About 2 cups (500 ml)

2 cups sunflower seeds
2½ cups water
¼ bell pepper, cut into large pieces
4 dates
5 sun-dried tomatoes, soaked
a pinch of salt
juice of one lime
optional: garlic

Mix sunflower seeds with water in the blender until they obtain a creamy consistency. Cut the peppers into large pieces and mix them with the other ingredients until well blended. Taste, and add garlic if you like.

Lunch—Delicious Salads and Creamy Dressings

The body is now ready for some heavier food. Now it's time to eat nuts, seeds, and oils, or avocado, combined with a large salad. Keep in mind that lunch should provide you with a light and happy energy and should leave you feeling wonderfully satisfied.

Lunch is based on leafy greens. Vary according to the leaves and lettuces available. With your salad you may serve any of the following dressings. If you do not have time to make a dressing, take an avocado and drizzle with a tablespoon of olive oil and a dash of lemon. You can also replace the dressing with dried onion crackers. The reason that you should choose either avocado, dressing, or crackers is that there is too much fat if you take more than one of the options, and too much fat can slow down your digestion.

With the salad, you can eat pickled vegetables and seaweed—experiment to see what your favorite kinds are. If you need extra salt you can use an herbal salt or tamari.

IDEAS FOR YOUR LUNCH SALAD:

* leafy greens
* cabbage and red cabbage
* celery
* carrots
* tomato
* peppers
* zucchini
* cucumber
* snow peas
* radishes
* avocado (excluded if you have a nut or seed dressing)
* cauliflower and broccoli
* seaweed
* sauerkraut, pickled carrots, beets, red cabbage, cucumber
* lemon and oil dressing
* sprouts and shoots

Pine nut dressing

Serves 2

Creamy and delicious for both lettuce and zucchini pasta!

½ cup (100 ml) pine nuts
2 tablespoons olive oil
1 tablespoon lemon juice
3-4 tablespoons water
a pinch of salt

Pulse pine nuts in a food processor until they are finely ground. Add olive oil, lemon juice, water, and a pinch of salt. Process until you have a dressing.

Works well with romaine lettuce, shredded or sliced carrots, tomatoes, and cucumber. May also be served with seaweed, sauerkraut, and onion alfalfa sprouts.

Avocado and dill sauce

Serves 2

A real summer dressing that can also be eaten as a soup. If you like the taste, just make a bigger batch.

½ cucumber
½ avocado
1 sprig of fresh dill or
    1 teaspoon dried
2 tablespoons water
lemon juice and tamari, to taste

Peel and seed the cucumber. Mix cucumber, avocados, dill, and water in a blender. Season with tamari and lemon.

Guacamole

Serves 2

Dip your lunch! Make guacamole and dip celery sticks, carrots, and cucumber.

2 avocados
2 garlic cloves
1 teaspoon lime juice
1 red onion
Himalayan salt and black
   pepper, to taste

Mash the avocado, squeeze the garlic, and add the lime juice. Mix well. Chop the onion finely and mix in. Season with salt and pepper.

Indian dressing

Serves 2

This dressing contains turmeric, which according to research is said to do wonders for the joints. About a teaspoon a day of the golden powder makes your body wonderfully supple.

½ cup (100 ml) pistachio nuts
¾–1 scant cup (150-200 ml)
   water
1 teaspoon turmeric
½ teaspoon cumin
1 teaspoon chili powder
1 tablespoon lemon juice
½ teaspoon salt

Mix pistachios with water. Add the spices and blend again into a creamy consistency. Taste and add more seasonings and water as needed.

Cilantro dressing

1-2 servings

You can make this with sunflower seeds or a creamier version with cashews.

½ cup (100 ml) sunflower
  seeds or cashews
1 scant cup (200 ml) water
1 tablespoon lemon juice
¼–½ cup (50-100 ml) fresh
  cilantro
a pinch of salt
½ avocado

Pulse sunflower seeds or cashews in a food processor to a fine flour. Add water, lemon, ¼ cup (50 ml) cilantro, and a pinch of salt and mix until blended. Add avocado and blend again. Taste and add more cilantro if needed.

Raw tahini dressing

Serves 2

I am a tahini lover and to smother a salad with tahini dressing—that's love!

1 onion or ½ small leek
⅜ cup (75 ml) sesame seeds
⅜ cup (75 ml) water
1 teaspoon lemon juice
1 teaspoon tamari
1 clove garlic
½ teaspoon basil, dried

Chop the scallions or leeks. Place all ingredients in blender and blend until creamy.

Apple and carrot dressing

1-2 servings
Works well with spinach leaves and celery sticks!

½ cup (100 ml) almonds
1 scant cup (200 ml) water
1 apple
1½ cup (300 ml) grated carrot
2 teaspoons lemon juice
a pinch of salt

Process the almonds in a food processor to a fine flour. Add water. Cut the apple into big chunks and mix with the grated carrots into a creamy consistency. Season with lemon and salt.

Pumpkin seed dressing

1 serving
The simplest dressing!

¼ cup (50 ml) pumpkin seeds
¼ cup (50 ml) water
1 teaspoon name shoyu or tamari
¼ yellow bell pepper
lemon juice to taste

Mix together all ingredients to a creamy dressing.

Green olive dressing

1-2 servings

This is a dressing I make over and over again. You can try making it with black olives if you like. The result is equally great!

¼ cup (50 ml) green olives,
   with or without pits
½ cup (100 ml) olive oil
¼ cup (50 ml) macadamia nuts
about ½ tablespoon lemon juice
a pinch of salt
¼ bunch of fresh basil

Prepare by soaking the macadamia nuts for about 8 hours.

Pit the olives. Mix the olives with half of the olive oil till well blended. Add the macadamia nuts, lemon, remaining oil, and salt. Mix again. Add the basil and blend into a smooth dressing.

Onion crackers

Make crackers to have with your lunch salad. If fresh red onions are in season, then you can also use the tops.

1½ cups (300 ml) pumpkin seeds
½ cup (100 ml) flax seed,
   soaked
½–1 red onion

Prepare by soaking flax seeds in 1 cup of water for 4 hours. Pulse pumpkin seeds in the food processor until they are finely chopped. Add the soaked flax seeds and process again. Add the red onion, cut in larger pieces, and blend into a batter. Spread on parchment paper or a teflex sheet in a thin and even layer. Cut into squares with a butter knife.

If you're making the crackers in a dehydrator, flip the crackers over after 5 hours and then allow to dry for another 5 to 10 hours. If you have a conventional oven, turn the crackers over when you can lift them off the parchment paper, and continue to dry until they are thoroughly dry. Break into cracker-size pieces.

Inspiration and Further Reading

Web pages:
www.thegardendiet.com
www.renegadehealth.com
www.rawreform.com
http://en.wikipedia.org/wiki/Raw_food

Books:
Victoria Boutenko, *Green for Life*, North Atlantic Books, 2010.
Gabriel Cousens, *Rainbow Green Live-Food Cuisine*, North Atlantic Books, 2003.
Harvey and Marilyn Diamond, *Fit for Life*, Grand Central Life & Style, 1986.
Natalia Rose, *The Raw Food Detox Diet*, William Morrow & Company, 2005.
Dr. N. W. Walker, *The Natural Way to Vibrant Health*, Norwalk Press, 2008.
Ann Wigmore, *Live Food, Health Food*, 1997.
David Wolfe, *The Sunfood Diet Success System*, Maul Brothers Publishing, 2006.
Dr. Robert Young, *The pH Miracle*, Warner Books, 2002.
Susan Powers, *Rawmazing*, Skyhorse Publishing, 2012.
Ulrika Davidsson, *Raw Food Detox*, Skyhorse Publishing, 2012.
Mimi Kirk, *Live Raw*, Skyhorse Publishing, 2011.
Jason Manheim, *The Healthy Green Drink Diet*, Skyhorse Publishing, 2012.

Contact the author:
Erica Palmcrantz Aziz, raw food inspiration
Contact: www.rawfoodbyerica.se

Many thanks!

To my husband, Sam, and our daughter, Saga, who teach me about life's magic and love.

To my mother, who is always there as chief taste tester and sounding board, full of maternal love.

To Irmela Lilja for her wisdom and wise words on the way.

To Susanne Hovenäs for her warmth, feedback on the manuscript and brilliant portraits in the book.

To the exuberant Anna Hult for her ability to visualize my thoughts and dreams in her beautiful images.

To my editors, Cecilia Lidbeck and Sara Carlsson, for support and insightful comments during the preparation of *Fabulous Raw Food*.

To designer Lina Bergström for her skillful sense of form and color.

The warmest thanks to you, who read this book and spread the power of raw food in the world by being excellent role models.

Recipe Index